lives to offer

Other books in the series

Practicing Discernment with Youth:
A Transformative Youth Ministry Approach

by David F. White

Branded:
Adolescents Converting from Consumer Faith

by Katherine Turpin

lives to offer

*accompanying youth
on their vocational quests*

dori grinenko baker &
joyce ann mercer

THE
PILGRIM
PRESS
Cleveland

From Joyce:
To Larry, my love and life partner in all that really matters

From Dori:
To Lincoln, with immense love and a heart full of gratitude

The Pilgrim Press
700 Prospect Avenue
Cleveland, Ohio 44115–1100
thepilgrimpress.com

© 2007 by Dori Grinenko Baker and Joyce Ann Mercer

Scripture quotations are from the New Revised Standard Version Bible, copyright © 1989 by the Division of Christian Education of the National Council of the Churches of Christ in the U.S.A., and are used by permission.

11 10 09 08 07   5 4 3 2

Library of Congress Cataloging-in-Publication Data
Baker, Dori Grinenko, 1963-
   Lives to offer : accompanying youth on their vocational quests /
Dori G. Baker and Joyce Ann Mercer.
      p.   cm. – (Youth ministry alternatives)
   ISBN-13: 978-0-8298-1726-3 (alk. paper)
   1. Church work with youth. 2. Vocation – Christianity.
3. Youth – Religious life. I. Mercer, Joyce. II. Title.
BV4447.B2155 2007
259′.23 – dc22

                                        2007020718

Contents

Foreword

For three decades the task of conceptualizing youth ministry has largely been left to independent commercial enterprises that have failed to recognize the importance of denomination, theology, ethnicity, class, and other cultural particularities for shaping Christian discipleship. In addition, youth ministry as it has evolved over these decades lacks significant critique of the shift in the social roles of young people in the second half of the twentieth century and into the twenty-first century, in which youth are increasingly ghettoized as passive consumers rather than treated as agents of faith influencing the common good.

Decades of domestication, marginalization, and trivialization of youth ministry by theology schools, denominations, and publishing houses has distorted our imagination of what counts as youth ministry. The image of youth ministry as trivial or pragmatic has left many hungry for youth ministry approaches that include social critique and engagement, theological sophistication, faith formation, and a genuine knowledge of and respect for the unique youth of today. The Youth Ministry ALTERNATIVES series has been jointly conceived by The Pilgrim Press and David F. White and Faith Kirkham Hawkins to address that hunger.

The Youth Ministry ALTERNATIVES series aims to clearly articulate approaches to youth ministry that embody social awareness and theological reflection and foster the distinctive gifts of youth for the church and the world. The series will highlight approaches to youth ministry that embody the following commitments:

1. **Dialogue with Living Communities.** This series will highlight approaches for fostering dynamic dialogue between the Christian traditions and youth and adults in living communities of faith.

2. **Deeper Understanding.** This series will engage this dialogue to deepen understanding of youth, theology, and youth ministry. Of particular interest is the wisdom emerging from a variety of underexplored sources that will be identified and interpreted, including the following:

   - the wisdom of youth
   - the wisdom of communities engaged in youth ministry
   - the contexts of youth, including their inner landscapes, communities, cultures, and physical environments
   - the resources of Christian tradition

3. **Transformative Practices.** From these conversations and the wisdom gleaned from youth, communities, and their contexts, this series will especially highlight a range of practices for engaging youth in ministry, such as:

   - doing theology and ministry with youth
   - taking youth seriously — their wounds, blessings, and gifts
   - mobilizing and enhancing youth agency and vocation
   - enhancing formation and transformation of youth as they journey in faith
   - articulating clear approaches to youth ministry
   - discerning a congregation's unique youth ministry

Girls and boys in contemporary U.S. culture tune in to many voices on their way to discerning vocation. Popular culture tells girls they should aspire to be sexy and thin. The video game industry markets a world in which boys are rewarded for quick, finger-activated response to perceived threat. During nationally televised sporting events, slick commercials romanticize military service. Olympic replays disproportionately highlight bikini-clad volleyball players. Schools driven by standardized learning cut funding to the arts, while funneling resources toward creating better test-takers. Both boys and girls watch reality shows that glorify aggression, sexual commodification, and material gain. Voices screaming over these airwaves tell boys how to become certain kinds of men and girls how to become certain kinds of women. The voices create a "curriculum of vocation" that goes largely unchallenged. To counter this cultural curriculum, in *Lives to Offer: Accompanying Youth on Their Vocational Quests*, Joyce Mercer and Dori Baker propose a vision of youth ministry as a companioned walk with young people in search of vocation. In this vision, faith communities provide companions — parents, other adults, and peers — as faithful sojourners with youth in search of compelling ways to "offer their lives" in response to God's call. In this book, Dori and Joyce engage a theological understanding of vocational quest that involves simultaneously a "private" or inner discernment of individual gifts by a teen, and also as a deeply public quest, fostered within a community of others who also struggle to live lives of meaning in relation to God's call. This book will foster conversation about how parents, churches, youth ministers, teachers, and other caring adults can help facilitate meaningful quests for vocation in such a time as this.

DAVID F. WHITE AND FAITH KIRKHAM HAWKINS
Series editors, Youth Ministry Alternatives

Series editors Faith Kirkham Hawkins and David F. White are respectively Director of the Youth Theological Initiative and Assistant Professor of Youth and Education at Candler School of Theology at Emory University in Atlanta, and C. Ellis and Nancy Gribble Nelson Associate Professor of Christian Education at Austin Presbyterian Theological Seminary in Austin, Texas.

Acknowledgments

Because this book has been such a thorough collaboration between the two of us from the start, we begin by acknowledging some important people we *both* want to thank. Writing can be at times such lonely work. It is often difficult to find a listening ear with whom to share the burden of a belligerent idea. The process of jointly creating this book was a lovely relief. We experienced the joy of lobbing a half-formed thought and having it returned surprisingly complete. Laughter abounded. Collaboration was at times magical, eased by mutual respect and balanced by lightheartedness. So our first expression of gratitude goes simply to one another, but more mysteriously to the source of such grace, by which we found one another and this project at just this season in our lives.

Collectively we'd also like to thank the young people whose stories fill these pages. The high school students who took part in interviews through the Youth Theological Initiative (YTI) at Candler School of Theology opened their lives and stories in wonderful ways as teens, and again in their early adulthood as we conducted follow-up interviews with many of them. As we spoke to some of them years after their YTI experiences, they remained spirited conversation partners dedicated to exploring faith in honest and courageous ways. The young people we served in parishes, clinics, and other places of ministry likewise shared their lives with us. It is a privilege to have walked alongside them.

Under the leadership of David White and Faith Kirkham Hawkins, we began gathering with other research fellows in 2004. This gathering provided time and space for our initial talks (and walks) about youth and vocation to take place. This extremely collegial group reviewed early chapters and provided many fruitful pathways as we approached the "mountain" of data YTI had collected in its first twelve years. We are particularly grateful to the insights shared by our friends Helen Blier and Don Richter along the way and for the Lilly Endowment's foresight in funding YTI, whose important work has helped shape new trends in youth ministry. In addition, we thank the Wabash Center for Teaching and Learning in Theology and Religion, and Kenda Creasy Dean and Faith Kirkham Hawkins for hosting a Wabash Center gathering of seminary faculty who teach youth ministry. This meeting was generative for each of us, and it was also the place we first met face to face and began to notice our soul connections in shared passions for the well-being of young people. Princeton Theological Seminary's Institute for Youth Ministry has been a fertile forum for both of us. Portions of chapter 8 grew out of Joyce's reflections on youth and vocation for the 2002 Princeton Lectures on Youth, Church, and Culture. Our friends at the Association of Professors and Researchers in Religious Education / Religious Education Association helped chapters 3 (nature) and 5 (film) mature by reading and responding to them. Chapters 4 (holy listening) and 6 (girls) were likewise strengthened by appearing in the November 2005 volume of the *Journal of Youth and Theology* of the International Association for the Study of Youth Ministry.

Writing can occasionally be blissful, but at other times it is little short of torment. There are few people who actually have the power to make writers' lives bearable in such times. Our editor, Ulrike Guthrie, surely is one such person. Through deft exercise of her craft, she improves our ability to communicate with our readers, and also enriches our lives in many other ways with her professional skill, personal warmth, and friendship. Thanks again and again, Uli.

Our individual acknowledgements follow.

I (Dori) would like to thank the web of support that allows me to exist happily as a writer and professor-at-large. This includes my students at various seminaries, most particularly the summer 2006 class on human development at Union–PSCE in Richmond, Virginia, who helped me hone ideas about vocation across the lifespan. Former students Jason Stanley, Brenda Faison, Wendy McCaig, and Angie

Williams remain important conversation partners. I thank my friend and mentor Jack L. Seymour for companionship along my walk of vocation. My heart is grateful for ongoing encounters with other Garrett colleagues, including Adolf Hansen, Margaret Ann Crain, Dwight and Linda Vogel, Reginald Blount, and Evelyn Parker.

My writerly friends Myral Polikoff, Kelly Wheeler, and Lana Lowe gifted me by reading and commenting on early chapters. My circle of silence — graced by the presence of Anne Gibbons, Mary Ann Lippincott, Kaye Edwards, and Janice Monroe — more than once helped me believe. Members of Lane Memorial United Methodist Church of Altavista, Virginia, and Altavista Presbyterian Church have consistently shared their children and their stories with me over the past eight years, enriching me largely. The Altavista YMCA and Arts Council provided a "third space" for lively chats, as did Wednesday nights at the home of Glenn and Debbie Berger.

Old seminary friends Wanda and Germano Streisse-Diefelt and their daughters Carolina and Gabriella, as well as the Andrews family (Thom, Laurel, Ryan, Evan, and Cameron) all drove cross-country to share family vacations while this project was simmering. Watching how each of these forty-somethings and their teens and tweens live into their unique vocational gifts quite carefully supported my vision for this book, as did Wanda's reflections on teaching about vocation at Luther College in Decorah, Iowa. Her students Lucas Westby and Joe Svendsen graciously agreed to share their journal entries on vocation with me.

My family lives surrounded by trees, which in the winter, leaf-bared, open a horizon that is daily painted in orange, pink, and purple sunsets. I am grateful to live in a place where the sky is my regular companion and nature is close at hand. However, living far away from a seminary library and conversation partners exacts a cost. I am deeply grateful to my husband, Link, for caring so much about my work and the lives we create daily. I thank my daughters, Erin (friend of butterflies and justice) and Olivia (always contemplating her place in the cosmos), for thriving despite the absences my calling often requires.

I (Joyce) appreciate the wit, energy, and critical attention of students in my courses on "Ministries with Youth," and "Youth, Church, and Culture," in past years at San Francisco Theological Seminary and now in my new "vocational home" at Virginia Theological Seminary. I am grateful for supportive colleagues in San Francisco who understand my passion for research and writing, and therefore why I would rather move across a continent than leave either behind, with special thanks to Elizabeth Liebert, Charles Marks, Dan Hoggatt, Lewis Rambo, Carol Robb, Tito Cruz, Boyung Lee, and Philip Wickeri. Many new friends and colleagues in Virginia have eased the stress of writing a book amid a cross country move and adjustments to a new institutional culture, especially Barney Hawkins, Roger Ferlo, Tim Sedwick, Jacques Hadler, Amy Geary Dyer, Ruthanna Hooke, Judy Fentress-Williams, Kate Sonderegger, Tony Lewis, John Yieh, and Michael Battle, to name only a few of those whose generous hospitality has graced my relocated life.

Friends Jonathan Lee and Esther Kim provide so many kinds of support and care, as we all try to figure out how to do the juggling act of work, church, and parenting as sites for living out vocation. Two congregations with "old" in their names — in San Francisco (Old First Presbyterian Church) and in Alexandria, Virginia (Old Presbyterian Meeting House) — have been congregational contexts for me and my family in practicing our faith. Mallory Price (Brownie leader and soccer coach extraordinaire) embodies what it means to "be there for *other peoples'* kids," and I sure am glad she and her family have been here for mine. Karen-Marie Yust, besides being a darned good practical theologian, has walked with me through several of life's deserts, and lingered over several of life's feasts — during the writing of this book. Tim Van Meter was helpful in several conversations on social theories of knowing in C. A. Bowers and Gregory Bateson. Chuck Foster, Letty Russell, and Jim Fowler each continue to be significant mentors, long-distance conversation partners, and friends. My extended family — Walt and Cathy, Jack, Kyle and Rebekah; Barbara; and my dad, Virgil — bring humor, crazy energy, and a sense of connection "from generation to generation." My immediate family — Larry, Andrew, Micah, and Sarah — are the most important reasons I write, even though at times doing so burdens them more that it blesses. I am grateful for the life and lives we share together.

Chapter 1

Finding lives of meaning

Individual quests carried out in the company of friends

During a recent Sunday morning worship service, a pastor called forward eight robed students who were graduating from high school later that day. Giving each graduate a moment to shine, the pastor introduced the student, said a few words about his or her accomplishments, and asked about their future plans. When he got to the third student, the pastor indicated that the congregation was especially proud of Mark, who had graduated fourth in his class. Mark stated that he would be going to a nearby state university the following year to study physical therapy.

"Physical therapy?" The pastor exclaimed. "Why, you could be a doctor!"

The pastor moved on to the next graduate.

The friend who told this story was troubled. Her husband is undergoing treatment for prostate cancer. "If all the gifted students become doctors," she said, "What a sorry lot of nurses, physical therapists, and x-ray technicians we'll have." Highly aware of the need for many areas of specialization within the field of medicine, she was disappointed in her pastor for seeming to support a consumer-driven model of vocational discernment which seemed to place money and status above an appropriate response to one's particular gifts, desires, and calling.

1

Living the good life

This book is about those gifts, desires, and callings. Mark is not alone in finding his aspirations called into question by a community of anxious watchers. Though well-meaning, his pastor was giving voice to a host of problematic ideas about "what really matters." Parents, teachers, and other adults value for their youth a constellation of hopes and dreams, with promises of the "good life." This set of promises is implicitly communicated through multiple "teachers." We are calling this a curriculum of vocation, and we want to challenge it.

Set within a consumerist culture, this curriculum of vocation teaches that reward comes from making money, rather than from making a meaningful contribution. It teaches that true happiness comes from having expendable income, rather than living in ways that tap into deep joy. The ability to buy, consume, and possess is lauded over the ability to give, nurture, and enjoy creation. The measure of success is how well one asserts self-interest, not how well one's individual acts contribute to a common good. This implicit curriculum generates an ethic that bears little resemblance to the ways of Jesus. Indeed, it sometimes fosters life practices that starkly oppose *his* vision for humanity.

Young men and women in contemporary U.S. culture tune in to many conflicting and confusing voices on their way to discerning vocation. Voices within popular culture tell girls they should aspire to be sexy and thin, as well as "smart, strong, and bold." The video game industry markets a world in which boys are rewarded for quick, finger-activated response to perceived threat. During nationally televised sporting events, slick commercials romanticize military service. Olympic replays disproportionately highlight bikini-clad volleyball players. Schools driven by standardized learning cut funding to the arts, while funneling resources toward creating better test-takers. Both boys and girls watch reality shows that glorify aggression, sexual commodification, and material gain. Persistent messages over the airwaves tell boys how to become certain kinds of men and girls how to become certain kinds of women. The voices create a pervasive and persuasive curriculum of vocation that goes largely unchallenged. In addition to hearing a version of it from his pastor, Mark hears it from teachers, guidance counselors, movie scripts, websites, radio morning shows, and peers. These voices might seem to be saying, "You can be anything you want to be when you grow up," but hidden beneath these words are messages begging him to comply with certain images of adult male success.

Yet over against the din of consumerism, materialism, violence, and militarism, other voices speak. These voices recall an alternative curriculum of vocation, whispered in the cadences of an ancient chant. Teasing it out of the quiet spaces where it lies dormant, we want to revisit this alternative. What does our faith teach us about how to live the Good Life? Might it not call us to walk a simple path that seems overgrown with tangled vines, but in fact invites a wandering spirit?

The primary audience for this book is caring adults who work alongside youth in churches, families, and communities. As youth workers, we carry an "invisible backpack" of resources that inform our practice. Things such as the games we play, the movies we watch, the trips we take, and the ways we process all of these experiences are the "stuff" in our backpack. Some of it no longer fits.

In this book, we want to refresh the contents of the youth worker's backpack. We hope to fill it with some alternative, vital, and life-giving tools necessary to seek an authentic Good Life in keeping with God's good news. This Good Life is something we all want: the adults *and* the youth with whom we walk are all on this journey together. For young people like Mark, who desperately want a life that matters, genuine alternatives are essential.

An alternative curriculum

Genuine alternatives to existing models of youth ministry are essential because we live in a world at risk, where war follows upon war and hunger is all too prevalent. We hope for prophets, sages, healers, and activists who will sense an urgent call, find a community of support, and respond with lives to offer. We believe communities of faith are deep wells from which such lives may spring. Young people are hungry to offer their lives in ways that can make a difference in a world such as this. But to do so they need resources in *their* backpacks. Those resources derive from retrieved notions of vocation, community, gender, adolescence and grace. They include:

- Vocation: An understanding of life as gift from God, in which struggle and celebration hold hands, as each person discerns the purposes to which they are called.

- Community: Companions with whom to share their walk, discovering nuances they might not find alone.

- Gender: Freedom to imagine and negotiate life's details — who will take out the garbage, who will mow the lawn, who will pay the bills, and who will stay home with kids — across norms still deeply engrained, despite movements toward gender justice.

- Adolescence: A sense of the teen years as vital and filled with present value, rather than a holding pattern while awaiting "real life" as an adult.

- Grace: Wide margins of error in which to try on various roles, make mistakes, learn from failures, and still be loved.

We believe God's people — those still growing and those already grown — have lives to offer to a world in need. Youth ministries in mainline denominational churches are perfectly situated to help people discover how they can change the world, and some of them are doing so, remarkably well. But the focus of ministry with young people over the past thirty years has often drifted farther and farther from equipping people to serve in ministries of peace and justice, and instead has focused more narrowly on notions of personal salvation. This emphasis sometimes limits a wider view, in which, as John Wesley wrote, "the whole world is our parish" and all of life aches for connectedness. We hope this book will infuse contemporary ministries with fresh air, expanding their visions to encompass the distinctive gifts of progressive, Protestant theology, especially its signature focus on vocation.

Walking buddies: Who we are

The authorial "we" voice in this book refers to Joyce and Dori, two women who hope for a world in which all human beings might flourish.

We are mothers. We are teachers. We are clergy. We are activists. We are feminist theologians and professors of youth ministry, sharing a deep concern that the past decades' conversations around gender and justice bear fruit in the lives of today's teenagers — both male and female. Joyce currently teaches pastoral theology at an Episcopal seminary near Washington, D.C. She spent the past six years on the West Coast, teaching in an ecumenical seminary context where bold experiments in youth ministry and spiritual practices are giving birth to new models of church. Dori lives on the East Coast and has spent the last decade shaping pastoral practices that take seriously the stories of youth. We are both mothers of pre-adolescent girls and boys. Our own hopes and visions for them are written between the lines of these pages.

Through the years, we have practiced various occupations: newspaper reporter, social worker, hospital chaplain, missionary, pastor, seminary professor, arts educator, volunteer coordinator. Each of these "jobs" reflects concrete moments in a larger mosaic we are still creating. We call it vocation. That mosaic encompasses not only what we do for money, but all we do as God's called people. All of these pieces of our identities come together in this book around a common hope: that faith communities might be hospitable environments within which young people and adults might hear God's call on their lives and respond.

When we get together, the first thing we do is take a walk. We've walked the Connecticut countryside, hills ablaze with fall colors.

We've walked a southwestern river trail at daybreak, and a pacific northwestern redwood forest with the faithful companionship of Joyce's dog Sandy. We've walked Alexandria, Virginia; Toronto, Ontario; and the suburbs of Atlanta, Georgia — often getting lost, but always finding our way home. For each of these walks, we pack a backpack with the things we need — water, trail mix, a map, sometimes a cell phone. Also we carry ideas — snippets of a conversation with a colleague, a recent NPR broadcast, the latest novel one of us is reading, or a research report that arrived in yesterday's e-mail.

Walking grounds our imaginations. It puts us in a space to create new ideas, to challenge each other's perspectives, and to tell our stories — even as we breathe, feel the tone of our muscles, or wear a blister in a vulnerable spot. Miles of hiking together have given birth to a specific vision: youth ministry as a companioned walk shared by faithful sojourners in search of compelling ways to offer their lives in response to God's call.

Gentle eavesdropping: Other voices on the trail

On some trails, you have to watch out for roots. Partially hidden, they can trip up the unsuspecting. The terms "vocation," "adolescence," "gender," "community," and "grace" are concepts at the roots of our vision. Defining themes like this will help us chart the trail ahead, but such definitions require immersion in concrete contexts. Mark and a few other friends help us reveal our understandings of these terms.

Mark is a Euro-American male adolescent who shared his vocational longing in the public space of Sunday morning worship. **Katherine** is a young woman who decided to pursue her dream of organic farming, rather than following her parents' footsteps into a medical career. **Maria** learned from her Central American grandmother an ethic of generosity that turned upside-down her view of materialism. **James**, a recent college graduate and high school history teacher, spends hours each week with the youth in his church, fostering their leadership skills and empowering their ministries.

These people, along with others we will introduce, help reveal some of the nuances of the adolescent vocational journey. They are young people on whose lives we've had the privilege of gently eavesdropping. Through research gleaned in a Lilly Endowment project for high school youth, conversations with youth we pastored a decade ago, and other windows on the lives of teens, we engage real-life stories of teens navigating the complex trails of growing up.[1] We meet:

- A young woman who — through her love of canoeing the wilderness of Canada — discovers a passion for biology. She becomes an environmental scientist and spends her summers slogging through the wetlands of Wisconsin, collecting dirt samples that help determine the impact of development on the mating ground of endangered species.

- A teenage girl who struggles with the failures of her congregation to live out its own theological convictions about who constitutes the Body of Christ. She goes to seminary, in preparation for ordination, so that she can work from within the church to reshape it into a more inclusive community of hospitality to all people.

- A young man who, after getting an engineering degree from an elite college, goes directly into the Peace Corps, intentionally delaying major purchases that he fears would make his life decisions financially driven.

What obstacles did these young people encounter on their way? Who was there to help them when the future seemed unclear? By

---

1. The formal research data for this book came from interviews compiled by Youth Theological Initiative (YTI) at Candler School of Theology at Emory University. YTI was the first of several seminary-based programs for high school youth begun by the Lilly Endowment in the late 1980s and beyond. It involved youth in four weeks of living in intentional community with other rising seniors who spent their days studying theology, worshiping, and reflecting upon Christian life together. A strong component of YTI is the invitation to become a public theologian, who can reflect upon the interaction between faith and public life. In addition to having access to transcribed interviews with young people during and after their immersion in YTI, we also conducted follow-up interviews with alums of the program.

keeping fresh vocational journeys in conversation with faith stories, we'll be able to ask questions such as these. What transformative moments in church, youth group, or summer camp help a teen discover vocation? How can a relationship with a positive adult role model help shape a future of meaning and purpose? Where are caring adults walking alongside young people as they seek a holy calling, over against an uncritical flow toward adulthood?

No one "does" vocation in the abstract. Mark, Katherine, Maria, and James live vastly different lives, lives that are embedded in particular communities, cultural contexts, and families. They are deeply situated in complex webs that both present opportunities and limit options. In order to talk about the lives youth offer, we need to describe what we mean by "vocation," "community," "adolescence," "gender," and "grace." These five themes inform what we leave in and what we take out of our backpacks as we prepare for ministry that draws people into the struggles and joys of finding lives of meaning and purpose.

Vocation: Beyond "What do you want to be when you grow up?"

With the word "vocation," we call forth ancient voices, steeped in Christian tradition. These voices, aching to be heard, speak of human personhood, nurtured in community and held in the light of God's grace. They speak directly to urgent questions youth are asking. When we bring "vocation" out of its secular meanings and into its theological fullness as life lived in response to God's call, we glimpse an alternative vision for youth ministry

"So what kind of work do you do?" This question often pops out of our mouths when we meet a new person. Our paid work matters. Similarly, when we meet a teenager, we ask, "So what do you want to be when you grow up?" This question implies a future trajectory focused around paid work. High school and college often revolve around preparing young people for the work force. Indeed, work does help to define who we are. However, to collapse vocation to this narrow definition restricts a fuller view.

In this book, we talk about vocation theologically, as the practice through which people offer their lives in response to God's call, amid a world in need. This means vocation is more than a job, more than a career, more than a religious office. Vocation, for youth, is not merely "what I want to be when I grow up," but is also "who I am and what I offer the world right now." Vocation, for adults, is not merely "the work that I get paid for"; it is also the mosaic of activities, paid and unpaid, that make up day-to-day life. Vocation is not just "the time I give to my church," but also time spent in the rest of the world, as Christians seek to live lives of integrity, meaning, and purpose in all that they are and do.

Vocation is, in the words of Old Testament theologian Walter Brueggemann "finding a purpose for your life that is part of the purposes of God."[2] Vocation refers to theological ways of making sense of everyday actions and experiences, framed in the light of a God who calls people to particular ways way of being in the world. Soccer coaches, Sunday school teachers, foster families — even soldiers and war protesters — all may be sorting through their actions in the world in relation to God's call. This theological view of vocation speaks to both the private or inner discernment of individual gifts, and also to the deeply public quest, fostered within a community of others who also struggle to live lives of meaning in relation to God's call.

call to a particular way of being in the world

Community: A companioned walk

Imagine the possibilities of a community in which experienced adults accompany young people on their walks of faith. What would it be like if youth, adults of all ages, and children really experienced the church as a community engaged together in Christian practices

---

2. Walter Brueggemann, "Covenanting as Human Vocation," *Interpretation* 33, no. 2 (April 1979): 126.

of service, hospitality, stewardship, and care of neighbor? What if these practices — along with prayer, worship, confession, and forgiveness — formed an intricate rhythm, so that each person was formed and transformed by the community of Christ? For many youth, participation in such a mentoring community of faith would radically reconstitute the role of the church in shaping identity.

Youth look to adults for help. Adults, however, often flummoxed in their own search for meaning, feel ill-equipped to guide the quests of youth. Quite frequently we hear youth workers reflect on the difficulty of finding adults to mentor youth. Beyond the excuse of being too busy, we also see a deep sense of inadequacy preventing adults from stepping forward. "If I don't have my act together, how can I help another?" these voices ask.

Sometimes seekers make the best guides. Though some adults seem to arrive once and for all at a balanced life of work and play that answers life's deepest longings, that is not usually the case. Most of the people we know find that the job disappears, "having it all" breeds despair, the marriage fails, or the children grow up, reopening old questions about where life's meaning resides. These people find themselves needing to "reinvent" their lives. In such a world, it is easy to eclipse vocation into the next marketable resume.

For us, decisions around how to offer one's life to the world are central to an alternative vision of youth ministry. In fact, we view the adolescent quest for meaningful life as a crucial opportunity for the church to engage in the kind of ministry Jesus embodied. That ministry, as Luke's Gospel reminds us, heals the lame, clothes the naked, gives sight to the blind, and sets the captives free. The church exists, not to maintain itself, but to form disciples for the sake of the world. Christian faith, then, transforms individual lives and equips communities to change the world through such acts as alleviating poverty, advocating peace, re-imagining urban landscapes, and fostering global compassion.

Youth, in this vision, might be both seekers and guides, prophetically engaging the congregation in authentic questions about its own life, offered to the world.

We envision churches as communities of practice in which believers accompany one another in living out their baptismal callings — callings that take them into pockets of brokenness and need in an at-risk, hurting world. We invite readers of this book to imagine with us a church in which adults are companions of young people in their vocational journeys.

Re-imagining youth ministry in this way might also engage adults in deep searching of their own life commitments. It will invite them to ask how one's way of making a living, spending free-time, raising children, setting aside college funds, and volunteering in the community grow out of a Christian theology of call.

We invite readers of this book to consider vocation as *the* central theme for youth ministry. When we gather in educational settings to reflect on life experience, we provide for one another sites of holy listening in which authentic selves may emerge. As we construct such spaces — during a mission trip, around a common meal, or after a deep immersion in nature — we may do so with our imaginations tuned to the Holy. Perhaps God sees unique potential in each embodied soul gathered here. Held in this light, a young person's emerging vocation takes shape as an individual quest best carried out in the company of friends.

Acknowledging both the private and public dimensions of vocation provide relief from the burden of hyper-individualism and the stress to overachieve. No longer is a teen on a solitary quest to figure out "what I want to be when I grow up" or even "who I am" in the here-and-now. We are on that quest together, implicitly and explicitly contributing to the back-and-forth processes that result in particular vocational expressions.

Personal vocation shapes the life of a community; and communities certainly shape the vocation of persons. Therefore how any of us offer our lives in love and service is never only private or public. Instead, it always involves a mutual process of shaping and being shaped. Youth who join faith communities join themselves into the particular vocational call of *that* community, even as they contribute to the transformation of that call. For example, Timothy and Emma were confirmed in an urban congregation with an active ministry to its homeless neighbors. Emma had a knack for hanging out with guests at the soup kitchen. Timothy, too, came to call these neighbors friends. Together, they became integral to that ministry, serving dinners and getting to know guests over dinner conversation. When tension between the homeless and neighboring merchants arose, this congregation had to get involved in the messy work of being neighbors to both parties. The particular energies of Timothy and Emma, advocating for their homeless friends with police officers and city officials, contributed to the congregation's ability to make sure the homeless people didn't become the scapegoats in this conflict.

In this way, we see Timothy and Emma's calling evoked by the vocation of the community. Likewise, the congregation's ministry changed because of the distinctive gifts Timothy and Emma brought. God's call for Emma and Timothy to use their gifts came as a present-tense call, inviting them to the church's ministries of justice and care *during their adolescence*. While some communities of faith treat the teen years as a period of preparation for discipleship, this congregation found its ministries reshaped by two youth in whom God was at work already.

Adolescence: *Walking in place or going somewhere?*

"Adolescence" is a highly charged word. It is a concept that is contested and sometimes confusing. We often are greeted with puzzled looks when, in our teaching, we define adolescence as the years between thirteen and thirty. Many seminary students look at each other, do the math, and realize that our definition puts them squarely *in* adolescence when they thought they had left it behind long ago.

When we explain that cultural changes in North America have pushed the edges of adolescence in both directions, back toward childhood and forward into the third decade of life, those students nod their heads in agreement. We see it driven back into the "tween"

years by the earlier onset of puberty and by heightened marketing aimed at recruiting younger consumers. We see it edging into
the "twenty somethings" as more people (at least, those among the
middle and upper classes) feel the need for graduate degrees to prepare them for a changing economy. And those who don't go on to
college and other further education but straight into jobs are increasingly living at home longer, much longer, unable to afford the steep
housing prices on low incomes. Given these changing markers of
adulthood, perhaps adolescence is best understood not as a particular
age range at all.

For the past century, adolescence referred to a specific time segment
of the human life span marked by certain cognitive, emotional, physical, and spiritual changes. These changes were described in terms of
developmental theories that located adolescence beyond childhood
and not yet within adulthood. In such a perspective, youth appeared
as hormonally driven alien life forms on their way to "real life" in the
future. Based on the premise of universal, biological stages through
which the human species moves — like the life-cycle of a butterfly —
these developmental models offered a vision of youth that informed
generations of ministry. In a way, the church treated youth as "lives
on hold."

Developmental models continue to be helpful in understanding
some aspects of youth. And yet our notion of adolescence has been
overly determined by them. Biologically driven stage metaphors fail
to account for social and cultural differences that also shape personhood. Adolescence looks quite different in different parts of the
world. For instance, a thirteen-year-old boy in a two-thirds world
context might be helping to support his extended family with full-
time labor, a marker of responsibility that signals adulthood. A youth
of similar age in some more affluent U.S. neighborhoods may face up
to ten more years of school separating him from "adult" responsibil-
ities. In such a vision, the more affluent U.S. youth may appear to be
on a treadmill, walking in place instead of engaging in real life.

In this book, we address adolescence within the context of varying U.S. cultures. Hardly monolithic, these cultures also evidence

multiple ways of being. And yet we can recognize some shared patterns, common themes, and markers of growing maturity as young
people in different contexts solidify commitments regarding spirituality, intimacy, and work. Together such commitments map an
identity.

When we use the term "adolescence," we are talking about a space
between two meanings. The meanings of childhood, driven by parental norms and expectations, may be falling away. The meanings of
adulthood, driven by the demands of work life, have not yet taken
over. While treated as a fact, adolescence is actually imagined. Adolescence was constructed to account for the gradual coming-of-age
both observed and required by modern societies. Instead of focusing
on adolescence as a problematic set of years in the human life span,
we want to evoke the image of adolescence as an opportune time
to engage in relationships with the elders of a community, both as
learners and as guides.

Gender:
Negotiating the faded "no trespassing" sign

The past three decades have radically reshaped gender's role in determining vocation. Around the globe, females are taking unprecedented
roles in public leadership. A female president, Ellen Johnson Sirleaf,
was recently sworn into office in Liberia. Chile's Michelle Bachillet
recently became the first Latin American female president who did
not inherit the post from her husband. We have witnessed the entire
career of the first female Supreme Court Justice in the United States.
Women travel alongside men to outer space and labor side-by-side in
the American armed services.

Men, on the other hand, are now freer than ever before to partake
in work formerly deemed female. Male nurses are no longer out of
the ordinary. Men can now choose to be primary caregivers in the
domestic realm, while their wives function as the primary breadwin-
ners. Couples with highly sought professional experience can create

flexible schedules, allowing both mother and father to be present during a child's early years without significantly affecting family income. Those with less lucrative jobs also find ways to let emerging priorities around family reshape their work lives. A realm of choice exists around vocation that was unheard of merely a generation ago. We should be celebrating, right?

Unfortunately, our brains, bodies, intimate relationships, and networks of support do not always have time to catch up with the rapid social changes that allow for emerging patterns of male and female interaction.

Twenty years ago concerted efforts to mentor girls into voice and vocation became mainstream. Born out of feminism, such efforts aimed to teach girls to be "smart, strong, and bold" and to compete with boys in fields such as math and science that had always been viewed as male dominated. Groups such as the American Association of University Women have successfully intervened in public classrooms, heightening awareness of the subtle ways teachers guided academic achievement based on skewed visions of gender limitations. Despite many gains, women still experience discrimination in the workplace. They still earn less than their male counterparts. They still bear much angst over choices about work versus child-rearing. Many women practice a weighty juggling of public and domestic workloads that seldom feels manageable, much less sane or healthy.

Meanwhile other shadows emerged. Amid all the efforts aimed at positively influencing the lives of girls, who was teaching boys to be men? Aside from conservative evangelical fathering programs, which often reassert traditional roles of patriarchy, there have been few mentoring strategies aimed at boys. For the first time ever in U.S. history, boys are less likely than girls to gain admittance to college. Some authors have identified a "loser" mentality in which boys sense a limiting of future horizons and make subtle choices that accumulate into failure.[3]

---

3. Robert Dykstra with Allan Cole and Donald Capps, *The Spirituality of Boys: Losers, Loners, and Rebels* (Louisville: Westminster John Knox, 2007).

Where once there stood a "No Trespassing" sign on the borders of gender, now there is a faded rectangle reminding us that once impermeable boundaries are gone. What constitutes the "good life" for males today? Might we not guide boys to grow into smart, strong, and gentle men, gifted with emotional availability and skills for intimacy, as well as skills for succeeding in the marketplace? Likewise, what constitutes the "good life" for females? Might we not help young women listen to their inner voices — voices that might honor both their God-given potential for service and action in the world, as well as the biological gifts that accompany child-bearing? Might we not find ways to encourage men and women to honor both the still small voice within *and* the external voices of trusted companions who affirm calls and bestow blessings on the way?

Grace: It's not a race, and there's no finish line

Today's young people surely are among the most tested, evaluated, and assessed generation in recent history. They participate in competitive sports as preschoolers, and are tested to see if they meet state standards for learning before leaving kindergarten. Much of their elementary school curriculum focuses on test-taking skills to prepare them for a future of standardized testing in high school and college admissions. In the educational context of the United States and other countries, children and youth learn to equate their worth as persons with their abilities to achieve. Two teens, debating the value of their church's confirmation class, illustrated this well as one said to the other, "How important can it be when there's no test?"

This achievement orientation socializes adults and youth alike to understand human purpose and worth largely in terms of individual achievement. No wonder we Christians in contemporary U.S. churches seem to have so much trouble with the idea of grace! With grace there is no test. Life is not a race, and there is no finish line.

When we think about vocation from a standpoint of grace, we remember that our particular set of gifts and abilities is not earned by hard work alone, if at all. Some of our gifts — of a convivial personality, of mathematical prowess, of lithe beauty on the dance floor — come purely by chance of birth, inheritance, or quirk. Likewise, they don't belong solely to us. A community fulfilling its baptismal vows nurtures the seed of beauty within each child, and receives the benefit of that seed's fruition in the world.

A friend recently went to her sixteen-year-old son's debut as a director in a one-act play performed in the church basement. She and the other parents dutifully attended, expecting to suffer a bit through an amateur performance. To their surprise, the play was delightful and provided a night of supreme entertainment. Evan, who is not a joiner and has spent his life at the fringe of his family's churchgoing, nevertheless had found welcome in the church as a place for pursuing his talents. The times Evan had volunteered to run the sound booth in worship, made props for Vacation Bible School, and been car-pooled to endless rehearsals at the civic youth theater could all be celebrated that night as the community witnessed (and reaped the benefits of) the mastery of his chosen craft.

Sometimes kids fail. Despite natural abilities, despite years of lessons, despite "helicopter" parents hovering over them — there are times in adolescence when one's hopes and desires fall flat. An audition flops. A championship baseball game is lost because of one dropped ball. Worse, addictions or poor choices in relation to drugs, sex, alcohol, or violence cause a young person to swerve, sometimes with dire consequences.

It is at this moment that grace intervenes. In hard times, young people must consistently hear the voice of love telling them it's not about what you do, but who you are. A circle of friends that surrounds the brokenhearted (particularly when parents may be unable to do so) with assurance of worth in the sight of God and God's people is surely a treasure in a society deeply tainted by "achievement fixation." This kind of holding environment, which at times needs to exhibit the patience of Job, is the kind of community Jesus embodied and commissions us — his disciples — to make real.

Embodying this kind of community sometimes comes at great cost, because sinfulness is seldom solitary. Living as people touched by God's grace can empower us to confront the systems that keep people in cycles of failure.

The path ahead

In this chapter, we have defined vocation, community, adolescence, gender, and grace. These themes run through the chapters that follow.

In chapter 2 we look at contemporary U.S. culture. What is "culture" exactly, and how is it training our young people? We explore the "curriculum of vocation" and propose four tenets of the Christian faith that emerge as critically important guides to young people who want to shape their lives according to Christ's approach to greed, compassion, creation, and reconciliation.

Chapters 3, 4, and 5 take a turn toward the practical. Given a society that often tells us that our goal in life is to be rich, thin, young, famous, secure, and entertained, what's the church to do? We take a hike deep into nature, where we experience what it means to be unplugged from technology and engaged in reflection with the holy amid a circle of friends. We take a long look at entertainment — in the shape of movies — that can move us into reflecting on God's creation and our actions within it. Last of all, we experience the quiet spaces inhabited by holy listeners, adults who take time to hear young people's deepest longings into speech, image, action, and possibility.

Chapters 6 and 7 direct our energy toward gender and relationships. Girls and boys approach vocation differently because of centuries of accumulated "shoulds" about gender. We devote a chapter to boys and a chapter to girls, looking at the dance between culture and biology, parents and peers, faith communities and schools. Can the church be a place that leads the way in reminding us to nurture friendships? Can it help loosen gendered expectations and norms, freeing all people to live lives that are more fully human?

In chapter 8 we describe a future possibility sometimes called the beloved community. In this view of Christianity, we hope toward a vision of human flourishing in which everyone has enough. There is abundant life, from which *no one* is excluded. If we do not believe God intends for the earth's inhabitants to die in a fiery apocalypse or waste away from ecological destruction, we must hold out an alternative hope, based in scripture and sufficiently enticing to redirect deeply embedded habits of living. This hope drives our passions toward creating churches that welcome the gifts of each young person and enter the blessed task of nurturing those gifts, for the now and future world.

These themes are pulled together in the Epilogue, which is a conversation with Dr. James W. Fowler, whose work on human development and vocation remains pivotal for a generation of practitioners and scholars of ministry.

Just walk it

On a recent Sunday, a group of adults accompanied a confirmation class on a guided labyrinth walk. It was the first time any of them — adults or youth — had walked a labyrinth. The first steps were tentative because the stones that marked the labyrinth were hard to discern on the forest floor. Amanda, a sixth-grader, stood fearfully at the entrance. The guide, trained at Chartres Cathedral, home of one of the most famous and oldest labyrinths, and steeped in knowledge about the ancient tool, told her gently, "Just walk it, Amanda."

Amanda kept a careful watch on the adult a few paces in front of her. "I was afraid I would get lost," Amanda said, when reflecting on the experience. "It helped to look ahead and see Mrs. Green turning the next bend. I knew I would soon be where she was." Even though Mrs. Green was also unsure of her way and tentative about her next steps, she provided valuable companionship to Amanda. She walked a few paces ahead, providing hope to one who was navigating the same path.

Such a companioned walk is a fruitful metaphor for youth ministry focused on vocation. Adults walk a few steps ahead, providing guides who are navigating the same path and who offer insights from their experience. Carving out lives of meaning and purpose poses particular challenges in contemporary U.S. society, for both youth and adults. There are moments when we must "just walk it" trusting the good path will unfold before us.

A more robust vision of vocation helps young people make the leap from the religion they learn on Sundays to the faith they walk each day. If the Christian story is to make a difference in the lives of youth and the world, it must translate into practices that give life meaning today, at various places along the path to a purposeful adulthood. The concept of vocation engages us in precisely that. It holds potential to interrupt worldviews steeped in materialism with counter-narratives, redirecting the energies and gifts of young people toward the healing of the world they inhabit.

Mark, the young man in graduation garb before his congregation, wasn't standing on square one of the board game of life. Visions of his future self had been emerging in fits and starts, fed here and redirected there, for many years. We don't "begin" our vocations. They begin in us, guided and initiated by a creator God who knit us together in the womb. Neither could Mark, at eighteen, know exactly what his vocational life will look like at twenty-eight, thirty-eight, or fifty. We don't always get a clear glimpse of our purposes, fixed or fleeting. Like a labyrinth, though, they may unfold before us as we move along the path. The image of walking that path in the company of caring, reflective companions is the hope underlying this book.

Chapter 2

Walking alongside

In the last chapter, we introduced to you the image of vocation in youth ministry as a companioned walk. Figuring out who you are and what you offer with your life is a daunting task, and yet one that need not be undertaken alone. As members of faith communities, all of us are perfectly positioned to walk alongside young people, noticing, naming, celebrating, and calling out their gifts. We can, in a sense, envision ourselves as "on vocation" with youth. But in order to do so, we must take along with us a strong sense of what's needed to sustain lives of meaning and purpose in today's world.

The church is not just a gathering of individuals who hold similar beliefs. Throughout history, it has functioned as a collective, which, when organized around a particular crisis, can reshape the way the world looks, acts, and evolves. This image of the church as an agent of social transformation is another way of thinking about the church as the body of Christ, sent forth in mission to an aching world. For this reason, in order to talk about the emerging vocations of youth, we must also keep in mind the historical events within which these youth are coming of age.

In this chapter, we draw attention to four tenets of the Christian faith that emerge from the voices of young people and that can serve adults companioning them on the walk of Christian vocation. These tenets suggest important correctives *at this particular time in history* when the environment, global inequities of wealth and health, warfare often based on religious difference, and rampant materialism define much of our reality.

We begin, not with the big and perhaps daunting global picture, but where most of us find ourselves — with a local and particular scene, the story of how one girl's emerging vocation was awakened and nurtured by a circle of caring watchers facing specific historical events. Listen to this young person's story of how her identity was gently evoked by her elders in the midst of escalating violence against blacks during the civil rights movement. Brenda, the woman who told this story from her adolescence for a seminary class assignment, is now in her mid-fifties and embarking on a second career as a Christian educator. Perhaps her story can help us imagine ways to become more able companions to the youth we know.

I slowly opened my eyes blinking them rapidly as I welcomed the sunshine streaming through my window. The wintry morning air was pungent with the smell of Maxwell House coffee, country ham, and freshly applied Old English furniture polish. As I tried to bury myself deeper into the warm ruts of the comfortable feather bed that had been my sickbed for the last three days, I remembered that this was the day that my grandmother and her friends would begin their annual three-day quilting bee.

Curious about the quilting bee, I convinced my grandmother that I was well enough and mature enough at twelve years of age to get out of bed and join the quilting bee ladies with my book and pillow. Before everyone arrived she told me that she expected me to be on my best behavior. "Good little girls," she said "are to be seen and not heard."

The ladies arrived around eight o'clock that morning laden with all types of food for their lunch including pound cake, chicken salad, sliced ham, and potato salad. I found it very peaceful sitting quietly observing them as they began the process of preparing the quilt. They all sat around the frame with needle and thread in hand and began to slowly glide the needle in and out of the quilt top with tiny, very even stitches. Conversations ranged from selecting appropriate quilt patterns to new recipes for pound cake found in the Almanac.

As the afternoon wore on the ladies' conversation turned to discussions about their individual faith journeys. This discussion led them into talking about the hardships of black people living in America, the civil rights movement, and Dr. Martin Luther King. They questioned the role of the church in the civil rights movement and commented on the need to stay in constant prayer. The room seemed to vibrate with tension as the women described their fears for their families as our community began the process of integration. There were whispered talks of the Klan visiting Sister Butler's father-in-law's house. Although the ladies agreed that integration was upsetting, they all saw it as the means for their children and grandchildren to receive the best education possible.

It was at this point that I was brought into the conversation by Mrs. Sampson, my grandmother's neighbor, "Brenda, what do you plan to be when you grow up?" I replied, "I'm going to be a nurse." "How wonderful," one of the other ladies commented, "We are very proud of you." "We know that you are doing very well in school, and in times like these, that is very important." My grandmother looked me in the eyes and very pointedly said, "We did not have the opportunity to go to school because we had to work, but you will have the opportunity to go to college." "Don't let anyone tell you that you cannot achieve and remember to keep God with you at all times," Aunt Eloise stated emphatically. "Be a good girl and get your education first, then look for a husband." "Amen" sounded from each of them around the frame.

Though the conversation shifted back to the topic of integration, I knew I would never forget the importance of that lazy afternoon's conversation. I'd been given a charge that I would carry out for the rest of my life.[1]

Despite her grandmother's reminder that good girls are seen and not heard, Brenda witnessed the group's actions speaking more loudly

---

1. Brenda Faison, unpublished class assignment for Aspects of Human Development, Union–Presbyterian School of Christian Education, Summer 2006. Used with permission.

than the stated social conventions. The older women in Brenda's circle of care were inextricably part of the crisis unfolding in their newspapers and their neighborhoods. As they acted out their own faith-motivated responses to the struggles for racial justice, they looked to Brenda as an active participant, not a passive bystander whose life was on hold. They gave her affirmation, and they gave her a charge, blessed by a resounding "amen." They called Brenda into the grown-up circle and attended to the importance of the young person and the future in their midst. While their hopes for her pointed toward a Brenda-to-be in the future, their affirmation focused also on the Brenda present among them now.

Unlike the way high school functions to put "lives on hold" for Euro-American teens today, education in the African American community has been a primary space of empowerment and opportunity. Thus, education historically has functioned in the black community as a crucible for social change. For this reason, it is all the more painful that today's high schools often fail young people and their communities by focusing solely on information retention, rather than on preparing critical thinkers for a changing world.

Like Brenda's circle of elders, thoughtful Christians today read the newspapers and engage their neighbors, noticing a confluence of crises that threaten human life. The cover of *Time* magazine warns us to "Be Worried. Be Very Worried" about climate change due to global warming. Pope Benedict XVI hastily apologizes to Muslim leaders for calling portions of their teachings "evil and inhuman" — a statement that escalated already high levels of religious hatred and intolerance between Christians, Jews, and Muslims. The United States shifts from being held in high esteem to being the non-aligned nations' object of scorn. We see Iran and North Korea's potential to wage nuclear war, and we daily awaken to heartbreaking news about casualties on all sides of the wars in the Middle East. In the midst of these global crises, we deal with friends experiencing debilitating depression, the plight of the urban poor brought home through the aftermath of Hurricane Katrina, and schoolchildren practicing weekly intruder drills.

Our world is in need, crying out for people who are prepared, as was the biblical heroine Esther, "for such a time as this." Might these realities of life be causing epiphanies of recruitment in the young people we know? Might we, as adults and communities, echo, feed, nurture, and ground these epiphanies?

Attuning our ears to the world's deep wounds

In his helpful book *Forgetting Ourselves on Purpose: The Ethics of Ambition,* Brian Mahan coins the term "epiphany of recruitment" to point to those inchoate moments of call that are either pursued passionately or allowed to be forgotten and swept away in pursuit of "success American style." These epiphanies of recruitment, Mahan theorizes, are moments when the veil of consumption and materialism that seem to define our reality are lifted.[2] A person glimpses a cohering purpose in life — and reorders her existence in keeping with that purpose. This tweaks Buechner's well-known image of vocation as "joining one's deep gladness with the world's deep needs."[3] Here the world's deepest needs call out *beyond* what we think we desire, to voice possibilities that may involve denying some of our pleasures or delaying some of our gladness.

Young people today are concerned about the deep wounds of the world. Some of them know very well the thinness and lure of culture's promises and prizes, but it is not easy to step out of the race. Young people need adults brave enough to stop ignoring the ear-piercing sirens of warning. They need adults who are attentive not only to young people's sense of call, but who are courageous enough to attend to their own whispered epiphanies of recruitment and be willing to interrupt their own endless sprints toward success American style.

If the church is to help young people answer the world's deep needs *today*, it is time to awaken certain perhaps hidden, but already

2. Brian J. Mahan, *Forgetting Ourselves on Purpose: Vocation and the Ethics of Ambition* (San Francisco: Jossey-Bass, 2002), 30–32.
3. Frederick Buechner, *Wishful Thinking: A Seeker's ABC* (New York: Harper & Row, 1973), 73.

present commitments within the Christian story. Highlighting these commitments will lead us to imagine concrete practices that help us embody them.

We hear within Christian teaching four counter-narratives to the culture's curriculum of vocation. These counter-narratives are:

1. **Care for the earth:** Despite frequent interpretations of the Christian canon to support destruction of the earth and its resources, *biblical witness* can engage us in an embodied spirituality that limits waste and fosters concern about ecological destruction, global warming, and climate change. As Christians, we are called to help create a world of ecological sustainability.

2. **Avid curiosity about other religions and diversity within one's own:** Although Christians are often steeped in believing that Christianity is the *only* way and therefore seek to proselytize the "other," *biblical witness* can engage us in a posture of openness, rather than defensiveness toward Jews, Muslims, Hindus, Buddhists, and those of other religions. Christians are called to seek fruitful conversation and joint action with those who hold alternative religious worldviews, as well as engaging in conversation with those who hold opposing visions *within* Christianity.

3. **Reconciliation of violent conflict:** Despite claims that certain wars are endorsed by Christianity, *biblical witness* can engage us in the very difficult work of constructing peaceful alternatives to escalating violence, close to home and around the world. As Christians, we are called to be peacemakers seeking opportunities to collaborate in the midst of fiercely competitive worldviews.

4. **A heart of compassion for all living things:** Despite the popularity of theologies of affluence, *biblical witness* and the prophetic voices of Christian reformers throughout the centuries remind us of our responsibility toward more equal distribution of the world's resources, so that all may flourish. As Christians, we are called to alleviate human suffering, loving our neighbors as ourselves through acts of service and confrontation of evil structures.

This often entails a countercultural move of rejecting rampant consumption and materialism, so that we can no longer conveniently turn a blind eye to such issues as HIV/AIDs in Africa and lack of clean drinking water in two-thirds world countries.

These counter-narratives may be hard for some to discern in our tradition, scripture, and experience, especially as Christianity has come to be interpreted within U.S. consumer and popular culture. Many people, dissatisfied with the marriage of Christianity and mainstream consumer culture, choose to look outside the Christian tradition, say to Zen Buddhism or Native American spiritualities, to find their more earth-based concerns addressed and turned into concrete actions. But if we look carefully, we can find such beliefs and practices supported within our own Christian story too.

Recently, we've seen renewed attention to the environment from churches across the theological and political spectrums. The "What Would Jesus Drive?" campaign of 2005, spear-headed by evangelical churches, followed by heightened awareness of global warming, contributed to a green church movement that seems well underway.[4] Given what folks of all political and theological stripes are already doing, perhaps we shouldn't have been so surprised at the enthusiasm with which youth workers in the Midwest responded to our workshop's presentation about these four tenets. "Yes!" said one participant, emphatically. "These are the issues my son is absolutely passionate about!" These tenets posed a roadblock, however, for another participant, who asked "But aren't these political stances? Aren't we as churches supposed to remain apolitical?"

As ministers who have served in pulpits and know the importance of caring for congregation members enough to both honor and challenge deep-seated partisan loyalties, we guided the group in unpacking each tenet, one by one. Together we named ways that each tenet transcends bipartisan politics precisely because each is essentially a *human* issue.

---

4. *www.pbs.org/moyers/moyersonamerica.*

Interestingly enough, just as these four themes emerged in our conversations with youth and young adults, a strikingly similar "agenda" made headlines through former president Bill Clinton's Global Initiative 2006. Despite its obvious affiliation with a prominent democrat, this project drew widespread bipartisan support, marked by First Lady Laura Bush's participation. During that international gathering, concerned citizens spent three days focusing on practical solutions to four global challenges, named as energy and climate change, global health, poverty alleviation, and mitigating religious and ethnic conflicts. The numbers from that gathering are significant: It produced 215 action-based commitments, backed by pledges of $7.3 billion, which includes a $100 million pledge to fight HIV/AIDS in Africa, a donation of 20,000 bicycles in disaster-torn Sri Lanka, and promise of 100 hours volunteered in an interfaith youth group. The initiative also solicited simple commitments from everyday people, such as: "I pledge to reduce my family's carbon footprint. We're building mini-greenhouse planters to grow more of our own food and buying what we can locally"; and "I have started a micro-credit health bank in Malawi with US$5,000. It matches loans to twenty to forty families for starting small businesses."[5]

These examples point to the interrelated nature of the four tenets listed above: caring for the earth is compatible with having a heart of compassion that stretches toward justice for all living things; a posture of openness toward the religious "other" dovetails with the desire to resolve conflict nonviolently. So these tenets are actually closely interrelated and all grow out of the conviction that God's love urges us to move toward justice in the here-and-now. Together they undergird a curriculum of vocation that provides an alternative to practices that are destructive and do not contribute to our humanness.

The world's deep wounds very much preoccupy our youth and young adults. This situation calls for good pastoral care and spiritual formation, which can help people create safe spaces in which to *be*, without feeling constantly beleaguered to *do*. In addition, it calls for

---

5. *www.clintonglobalinitiative.org*. Access date 12/04/06.

activism, particularly activism that is grounded in and grows out of a life of the Spirit. When churches act passionately to provide counternarratives to the scripts of environmental destruction, greed, religious hatred, and violence, we also tend to see youth reversing their steady flow *away* from church. If they truly feel invited to an alternative way of being, lived out in communities of compassion and care, we have seen that they find the Christian message offers just the food for which their souls hunger.

But, indeed, we must acknowledge that living by these tenets — particularly as guides toward our commitments, investments, and actions in the world — requires more than a bit of redirection in many of our well-meaning congregations. It requires concrete and compelling practices that lead to vocational flourishing.

The empirical study *Soul Searching: The Religious and Spiritual Lives of Teenagers* depicts a current generation of youth who have been well socialized into the Christian beliefs of their parents. But the form of Christianity they've inherited often bears strikingly thin resemblance to the norms of biblical tradition. While nominally Christian, these teens were hard-pressed to voice basic values of the Christian tradition, instead tending to reflect an approach to religion defined as "moralistic therapeutic deism" which applies a utilitarian, consumer mode of passive reception to their religious lives. Segments of this generation seem captive to a worldview in which buying and selling pervade relationships: the metaphor of the marketplace is reflected in nomenclature for sexual partners such as "friends with benefits," and in motivation for altruistic service collapsed to a line-item on a college application.[6]

Similarly, we find that many young people cannot articulate even a cursory description of a lived Christianity. One youth, preparing to enter his senior year of high school and raised in a Presbyterian church, was able to speak clearly about his church's tolerance for diversity, but when asked about the content of his faith, he could not

---

6. Christian Smith, with Melinda Lundquist Denton, *Soul Searching: The Religious and Spiritual Lives of American Teenagers* (New York: Oxford University Press, 2005), 162–71.

move beyond "There is a God and there is a heaven and there is a hell." When asked what his church upbringing taught him, he said "I was taught that you had to accept Christ and have a relationship with Christ." When pressed to describe what this means, he could not articulate a faith that went beyond prayer and church attendance. This portrait of some young people's articulation of "church" is underscored by the work of Christian education professor Kenda Creasy Dean. She points out that churches which fail to embody the passionate love of God through concrete practices in the world are in fact hardly worthy of a young person's investment.[7]

We don't want to hold youth solely responsible when they have badly skewed views of Christian tradition. To a degree they are simply reflecting what they have learned from their elders. However, there is a point at which young people think their own thoughts and develop their own ideas. On the cusp of creating their own reality and gifted with burgeoning cognitive skills, they begin to sift through inherited wisdom and contribute their own reasoned re-visioning. How does such re-visioning happen? How do we start off in a new direction? One church's sign suggested that, "The sign of God is that we will be led where we did not intend to go." Redirections often sneak up on us. Sometimes, as was the case with Brenda when she joined her grandmother's quilting friends, a circle of care is there to help awaken and bless these emerging calls.

With that in mind, in the rest of this chapter we gently eavesdrop on some vocational journeys, still in process. The stories that follow come to us formally and informally from a variety of sources: from interviews with YTI scholars; talks with former parishioners tracked down because their journeys intrigued us; conversations with young people at national denominational gatherings; media reports of innovative youth outreach; and a chance encounter with a former babysitter.[8]

---

7. Kenda Creasy Dean, Practicing Passion: Youth and the Quest for a Passionate Church (Grand Rapids, Mich.: William B. Eerdmans), 2004.

8. In the examples that follow, we focus on the aspects of vocation that tend to get lived out in the work one does for a living or the professional preparation for

As we listen in, we ask: how are these young lives being directed or redirected by God's call? Do young people give voice to a *spiritual activism,* a sense of desiring to make a difference in the world that grows out of and is nurtured by their Christian faith? Are churches today actively stirring up, nurturing, and sustaining such calls? If so, what aspects of the biblical tradition and Christian theology stand out as especially important guides toward healing the deep wounds of our time?

Taken together the stories that follow help tease out the ways in which young people are finding their calls awakened and nurtured by local congregations, church-related institutions, and a host of other faith-inspired organizations. Here we find hints of a curriculum of vocation that points to caring for the earth, crossing religious borders, making peace, and seeking justice based on compassion — all present within biblical tradition, but perhaps in need of a neon highlighter. Tracing the threads of connection between the ways these young people are offering their lives and the ways their Christian faith sustains them might help us know how to better nurture the youth we encounter.

Caring for the earth

When Holly Alley was six, she had an instinctual love for animals, especially horses, and believed that somehow her life would always revolve around them. Her parents supported her in this love and belief. She took riding lessons and eventually showed her own horse. When she was ready for college, she chose a school with a program in equine science.

Midway through her freshman year, Holly became disillusioned with the program. While it taught her to better care for horses, it did not help her explore a budding need to embrace a deeper ethic

---

such work. While acknowledging the importance of this aspect of vocation for the purposes of this chapter, we also want always to keep in mind that vocation is acted out in *all* aspects of our lives, including work, family, pleasure, and non-paid service.

of care for nature. "I realized that there is only one Earth. Nothing I was doing worked toward sustaining it."

After coming to this difficult juncture, she investigated other schools, finally transferring to Warren Wilson College in Asheville, North Carolina. There, she found a school that requires one hundred hours of service learning during a student's four years on campus. Students might tutor at a local elementary school, organize a fundraiser for Habitat for Humanity, repair the plumbing in a homeless shelter, or hand-feed an orphaned fawn at a nearby nature center.[9] But she found more: what most attracted Holly to the campus was its deep commitment to ecological stewardship. She chose to major in conservation biology, which is helping wed her love of horses with a larger vision for building sustainable communities.[10]

As part of her service requirement, Holly traveled to a small village in Mexico on a mission trip with members of the Presbyterian church of her childhood. There, her awareness of the poverty affecting the developing world deepened, as did her desire to find a way to address that poverty through her life's work. "The part of Mexico we visited was so dry and so poor. I was just really aware of the poverty, the water pollution, and the lack of any kind of environmental protections."

Holly's congregation paid for her trip, and the adults on the trip became trusted companions with whom to foster an alternative worldview to the one her peers often hold. "Outside of a family who was pretty proactive about reducing waste, I had little knowledge of poverty and injustice. I hadn't been educated about where my food was coming from," Holly said. "Now, when I travel, I pay attention to agriculture with an eye toward how we can improve people's lives and care for the earth at the same time."

---

9. *www.warrenwilson.edu.*

10. Warren Wilson extends its green philosophy to local churches through a program called Green Walkabout. Congregations tour the campus to see ways the college has partnered with the natural habitat and adopted environmentally sound practices, such as a cafeteria that serves free-range beef raised on campus and campus buildings made from toxin-free materials.

A trip to Tibet as part of a sophomore religious studies course continued to enlarge Holly's growing awareness of the interaction of faith with everyday life. This trip was also partially financed by members of Holly's church, who claim her work of exploring and befriending another culture as part of their witness to the world. One congregation member said of Holly, "Where Holly goes, we will send her. We want to finance and foster her presence in the world." For the members of her church, what Holly is doing is not simply spiritual tourism. It is a journey of mutual mission, in which Holly uses her gifts of hospitality to cross borders in a reciprocal ministry of education and healing. Impressed by the peacefulness of the Tibetan Buddhists she encountered, Holly returned to her own faith seeking meditative practices that might ground her active life. Her temporary home at a Presbyterian college nurtures continuity with the faith of her childhood while challenging that faith in ever-expanding ways.

The biblical witness of Genesis, in which God creates the earth, places it in the cosmos, and charges humans to care for it is one of the Bible stories Holly recalls and claims from the faith of her childhood — which otherwise consisted mostly of learning "how to be a good Christian" within small circles of friends and family. Now a wider vision of Christian call is accessible to her in young adulthood. This faith reaches out from notions of personal salvation to embrace an earth and its people yearning to be honored in daily practices that sustain a delicate God-given balance. Although she is sometimes disillusioned with the politics and corporate entanglements she sees within Christianity at large, she remains hopeful that her faith story will continue to nurture the call she is living out now and reaching toward in her future. Key in this has been the active support of her home congregation, who fulfilled their part of the baptismal covenant by creating a circle of caring watchers, ready to lend their presence and their financial support to help her fulfill her calling.

Although for Holly the Genesis creation story is at the heart of her ethic of care for the land, she knows very well that the Genesis creation story is also often implicated in the current ecological crisis because it is often interpreted to endorse human *domination over*

rather than *collaboration with* nature. It is for this reason important
to underscore the additional Genesis theme of Sabbath, which reminds us that humans are created to enjoy a covenant relationship
with God and nature that continuously engages cycles of rest and renewal. Sabbath is a process of returning to right relationship between
humans and all that sustains them.[11]

The biblical Sabbath-related customs surrounding the year of jubilee are powerful examples of how we might practically care for the
earth. Every half-century the Hebrew people celebrated the Sabbath
of Jubilee — a two-year period known as the Sabbath of Sabbaths.
During this time, slaves were set free, land was returned to its right-
ful owners, and the earth lay fallow. Jesus referred to the concept of
jubilee in his teachings at the synagogue in Nazareth, when he announced the day of salvation in the words of Isaiah.[12] "The spirit of
the Lord is upon me . . . to bring good news to the poor . . . to proclaim
release to the captives, recovery of sight to the blind, to let the oppressed go free, and to proclaim the year of the Lord's favor" (Luke
4:18–19). Jesus' deep relationship with the earth and its people is
also evident in scripture through his stories about planting and harvesting. The depictions of Jesus feasting are examples of the earth's
bounty — be it wine, bread, or fish — multiplying so that all may be
satisfied.

These biblical and theological traditions remind us that caring
deeply for the earth is not ancillary but integral to Christian faith.
This means we must move beyond expressing mere sentiments about
the earth to foster disciplined practices that heal and sustain God's
creation. Youth in search of meaning and purpose in their lives
receive God's call through congregations like Holly's that walk alongside them, putting into practice Christian commitments that care for
the earth.

---

11. Dorothy Bass, ed., *Practicing Our Faith: A Way of Life for a Searching People*
(San Francisco: Jossey-Bass, 1997).

12. Rosemary Radford Ruether "Ecofeminism and Theology" in *Ecotheology:
Voices from South and North,* ed. David G. Hallman (Maryknoll, N.Y.: Orbis, 1994),
203.

Crossing religious borders

On a Sunday morning in downtown Chicago, Garrett Bucks steps into a worship space that feels alien to him. He is accustomed to United Methodist churches of Montana, his boyhood home, and the silent Quaker gatherings of his college years. The praise band, auditorium seating, and video screen do not say "church" to him as would an organ, stained-glass windows, or a carved wooden pulpit. But Garrett is a border crosser, intent upon learning how Willow Creek — a mega-church founded in the suburbs of Chicago and recently expanding into the city — might speak to the likes of him, a twenty-five-year-old who teaches English at a refugee resettlement house and names the alleviation of hunger as a primary task of the church.

"I'm using myself as a guinea pig. Can somebody from a certain theological tradition be spiritually fulfilled in a place that's very different from what they've known?" Garrett asks. "What venues and what movements and what issues could organize folks across theological differences?"

Although many of the elements of worship at Willow Creek feel strange to him, Garrett fosters openness to moments when the veil of separation falls away. He shared a recent one. "The praise band was doing this song and in the middle of it, they did this bridge to 'God is good all the time. All the time God is good' that I remember from all sorts of white liberal church services of my past. It was the first moment of 'Wow, I feel like home right here.'" He found this moment profoundly moving, and likened it to delighting in the taste of a cheeseburger after months of traveling abroad.

What is the source of this avid curiosity, this desire to find the intersection of diverse expressions of Christianity? What is the passion that drives Garrett to seek the places where liberal Protestantism and evangelical Christianity might find common goals?

"There is a reason why we think big ideas. It is because we have an eye on the world," Garrett says. This "eye-on-the world" echoes a hallmark of the Youth Theological Initiative. The framers of this Lilly Endowment program set out to create a "cadre of public theologians," a cohort of young people shaped and formed by an intense experience of theological study wrapped in intentional Christian community, and thereby empowered to offer their lives in significant ways.

Garrett, a 1998 alumnus of YTI, caught this idea like one might catch a life-giving virus, spread through living in close quarters with people of diverse backgrounds. He can pinpoint almost the exact moment when he was redirected into his current vocational trajectory, admittedly still very much in process. A person who had experienced "the beauty of church youth fellowship at its best...a place of openness and belonging and acceptance, exactly what youth ministry should be," Garrett came to YTI because he felt sure he was called to ordained ministry. He may still end up there, he says, but in the meantime his vocation has shifted from focusing inward on the church, to focusing outward on the world. What Garrett found at YTI — particularly through the rigorous debate that followed a black nationalist sermon preached on the Fourth of July — was a new lens through which to view the world and his place in it. That lens has everything to do with understanding the public aspects of a lived Christianity.

"Right now, Christianity could not be more polarizing. There are so many good reasons why too many people do not feel at home in a church. But a church that is about something — a church that is about love, embodied and acted out in sometimes risky ways — is the kind of church that doesn't lose its young." Garrett says. "We're all craving something to be about. Right now, churches give their individual congregants very limited ways to be about something. You create something really wonderful as church when you transform yourself and what you are about into tangible actions in the world."

For now, Garrett gladly walks this vocational tightrope, trying to balance his "big ideas" with everyday acts of justice-making. He enjoys his daily work with some of the world's most marginalized people. In his spare time, supported by a community of other Teach for America veterans, he thrills to envision a coalition that draws from across the theological spectrum to give people creative and comfortable ways to live out their faith and actually start making discernible differences in poverty in this country and internationally.

Garrett forges a Christian faith with a public face. Jeff Jones is another who can be numbered among the "cadre of public theologians" that YTI energized. Jeff infuses his daily work life with lessons learned in face-to-face immersion with the thick, rich, highly particular stories of religious difference he encountered in the YTI curriculum — not in the classrooms it created, but in the random moments for which it allowed.

A lifelong Presbyterian and preacher's kid, Jeff grew up in the suburbs of Chicago, but never had a serious encounter with a Roman Catholic until he shared a dorm room with one for a month at YTI. "I remember one day my roommate was talking about the pope. He got so emotional talking about this brave, spiritual man. I was blown away that one living person could evoke so much emotion in someone who was so much like me, demographically." Jeff recalls. "Where does this come from? Why is this person — the pope — so important? I'm not sure I ever got the answer, but it gave me a different respect and understanding for the ways we interact with religion."

Jeff draws a direct line between his YTI experience and the work he does today as a producer for St. Paul, Minnesota's *All Things Considered* program on National Public Radio. During the last legislative session, Jeff was frustrated at the endless sound bites regarding a constitutional amendment against gay marriage. "I kept saying, I want to bring in people who can really explain the thinking on all sides of this matter — not to fight with each other, but to help the quarter-million listeners that we have every week understand the things they don't have access to in their daily lives," Jeff recalls.

The memory of his Roman Catholic roommate's admiration for of the pope fuels his desire to help create a better-informed democracy. Jeff's avid curiosity about the thick, rich, particular life stories of religious difference invigorates his professional life in ways he attributes to his YTI experience.

Anne West's story provides a third example of the impetus from within Christianity to explore religious diversity. Anne is a twenty-two-year-old college student whose faith has been formed by an annual trip to the United Nations, first as a youth with a group of other United Methodists from Virginia and now as a mentor with that same gathering.

Each year, the group picks a topic of public importance they wish to examine through the lens of their faith. Two years ago, the topic was world religions. Anne's memories of this event are specific and bodily. She remembers *wearing* a yamika. She remembers *taking off* her shoes upon entering a mosque. She remembers *seeing* the Torah being unrolled in the synagogue. She *smelled* the incense of a Roman Catholic church. She *put on* the veil and *kneeled* beside Muslim women in prayer. The experience took her beyond thinking and into bodily living a piece of the religious life of another.

"Before that, I thought there was only one path, and that was Christianity. We were on the right path, and everyone else was wrong." Anne reflects. "Now I see that God is connected to everything. All of the world's major religions view God as a supreme being. In that way, we are more alike than we are different."

We consider the kind of border crossing that Garrett, Jeff, and Anne engage in as an important part of the Christian vocation. Avid curiosity about different religious traditions can be seen as one important tenet — already present within Christian scripture, teaching, and tradition — that might help churches guide young people on their vocational walk. This poses a challenge to churches and Christian-influenced culture. Typically church teaches us to invest our energies in our own religious home rather than turning our eyes and ears to other paths. Garrett, Jeff, and Anne carve a way around these "shoulds" into the adventuresome undertaking of understanding the religious "other." The adult faith community — represented by YTI mentors for Garrett and Jeff and a denominational body for Anne — provided the crucial guidance that allowed this vocational expression to emerge.

Clearly, Anne's exposure to other religions did not dilute her Christianity; in fact, she has experienced a call to seminary. Rather, her Christianity deepened through her embodied encounter with other religions, and it changed in one very important way: it stopped needing to negate other traditions in order to be valid. Christians confident enough in their own religious truth are able to venture along new paths with Garrett, Jeff, and Anne without fear of losing a tentative faith. They are free to explore with their emotions, intellect, reason, and imagination, pondering why so much diversity of religion exists and what possible purpose such diversity might have. Perhaps God intends for just such diversity, some theologians argue. Or, given humanity's free will and God's ever-adjusting ability to urge divine-human union, perhaps the diversity of the world's religions are simply the backdrop for a much larger drama than we can envision.[13] In the words of Bishop Katharine Jefferts Schori, recently elected presiding bishop of the Episcopal Church USA, "We who practice the Christian tradition understand [Jesus] as our vehicle to the divine. But for us to assume that God could not act in other ways is, I think, to put God in an awfully small box."[14]

In a historical era that recognizes the damage done by proselytizing missionaries linked with colonialism, some Christians find it refreshing to look to the world's religions as potential windows to truth, rather than enemies to conquer or change. Garrett, Jeff, and Anne help us understand how caring adults might walk alongside young people who are drawn toward mending creation through practices that honor and explore religious diversity.

Making peace

Rudy Balles was a former gang member who was filled with frustration and anger in 1994, after losing a friend to gang violence. But

---

13. Eugene March, *The Wide, Wide Circle of Divine Love* (Louisville: Westminster John Knox, 2005), John Hick, *A Christian Theology of Religions: The Rainbow of Faiths* (Louisville: Westminster John Knox, 1995).

14. "10 Questions for Katharine Jefferts Schori," *Time*, July 17, 2006, 6.

then he met Rigoberta Menchú Tum, who won the 1992 Nobel Peace Prize for her work for peace in Guatemala. The encounter changed Rudy's life. Now thirty, he directs a Denver-based gang outreach center called GRASP (Gang Rescue and Support), which sponsors annual cemetery visits to remember those who died in gang violence, as well as hosting peer-run intervention and emergency assistance for at-risk youth.[15]

Rudy met Menchú Tum through PeaceJam, a Denver-based organization linking teens with Nobel Peace Prize winners. Like Rudy some years before, on September 15, 2006, three thousand teenagers converged upon the University of Denver to spend time with Archbishop Desmond Tutu and His Holiness the Dalai Lama. They were part of PeaceJam's "global call for action to the youth of the world" and its tenth anniversary celebration.

The goal of PeaceJam is to inspire a new generation of peacemakers who will transform their local communities, themselves, and the world. Chapters form in high schools, churches, synagogues, mosques, and community groups. Annually, each region studies one particular laureate, in anticipation of a visit from that person. The visits create a mirror in which youth can see their potential futures reflected. At the end of PeaceJam's anniversary gathering, Archbishop Tutu addressed the crowd: "I look at you, and I am in awe. You are the ones who are going to make this a better world. The fact of the matter is Nobel laureates don't come floating down from heaven. There was a time when we were very much like you."[16]

Is this just youthful idealism? Or is it part of a movement in the United States that is reaching out to youth of all socioeconomic levels, awakening them to the need for skills of peace-building and conflict resolution, and then equipping them for the part they might play?

While PeaceJam avoids grounding its vision in a particular faith tradition, a similar organization grows specifically out of the long tradition of Christian peacemaking. The Peacebuilders Initiative, based

---

15. *www.graspyouth.org.* Access date 1/18/06.
16. *www.cbsnews.com/stories/2006/09/17/ap/national/mainD8K6RTHG0.shtml.*

on Roman Catholic traditions, brings high school students onto the campus of Catholic Theological Union in Chicago for a weeklong immersion event in the summer, followed up with two weekend retreats over the next year. During that year, attendees create a mentored "peace project" that they launch in their home congregations.

The Peacebuilders Initiative, a sister program to the Lilly-funded YTI mentioned earlier, aims to teach the fundamentals of peace-building while respecting diverse political views. It presents a positive image of peace-builders, especially historical figures such as the late Cardinal Joseph Bernadin, who was a leader in ecumenical social justice issues. Young people learn to maintain hope, even while acknowledging the difficulties of nonviolent conflict resolution. Key in the program is the opportunity for youth to be mentored in their home churches by adults committed to peace advocacy. Drawing on young people's capacity to go beyond "the prevailing culture of consumerism and individualism," this program believes high school students want to find meaning in their lives, want to deepen their spirituality, and want to do good things for others. By grounding participants in prayer, reflection, and faith sharing, the program is raising up a new generation of leaders who are steeped in the traditions and practices of wisdom, peace, forgiveness, and reconciliation.[17]

Through this organization, the church is actively engaging young people to move beyond remote, care-taking images of God as "cosmic therapist" or "divine butler" — as were reported in the research on teens conducted by Smith and Denton." It is instead helping youth to envision an alternative community through which a fiercely compassionate God shapes people for the work of justice-building and peace-making.[18]

Peace-advocacy is also awakened in quieter ways, through individual paths. Shannon LeMaster, a part-time youth minister and recent college graduate found her vocation redirected toward issues of conflict resolution while she was studying to be a church musician

---

17. *www.peacebuidersintiative.org*. This website contains a valuable list of links to international peace-related institutions of the Roman Catholic Church.

18. Smith and Denton, *Soul Searching,* 165.

and Christian educator. As an overweight teenager who was forced to move frequently during high school, Shannon remembers the insecurities she felt each time she had to begin making friends in a new place. She struggled with disdain for her body, knowing those feelings conflicted with an inner knowledge of herself as a cherished, worthy child of God. As she investigated the discipline of conflict resolution for a college course, Shannon began to wonder about connections between her inner conflicts as a teenage girl and outward conflict she experienced in her church, community, and world. "At a basic level, if I have a conflict on my face in the form of a zit, I cover it up with make-up. Covering up conflict doesn't solve it, and often worsens it," Shannon says.

She was inspired to share her awareness of the connection between personal spirituality and global issues of peace-making by founding a group for girls. The group helps girls address issues of body image and beauty, while making explicit their connections to widening spheres of family, church, community, and world — places where conflict is an ever present reality and peace-building can be seen as a Christian practice.

PeaceJam awakens teens to the lives of well-known peacemakers, some of whom are also spiritual leaders, redirecting young people's energies toward achievable acts of peace in their own communities. The Peacebuilders Initiative equips and mentors teens in concrete local peace projects, inspired by the life of exemplary witnesses to the peaceful way of Jesus. Shannon's redirected vocation illuminates an emerging path of Christian leadership focused around conflict resolution that weds the inner life with action in the world. All three are undergirded by a desire to repair a false rift between personal spirituality — which addresses the individual alone — and a more communal spirituality, which seeks to live out the biblical mandate to foster connections of care with the weak, the oppressed, and the least among us.

Earlier in this chapter we named reconciliation of violent conflict as one important resource of the Christian faith to which we might pay closer attention if we are to help youth find lives of meaning.

The call to be peacemakers redirects faithful Christians away from placing inordinate emphasis on the sports arena or on the SAT score and toward a vision of justice for all grounded in the new heaven and new earth that Jesus' life and ministry inaugurated. This is a realm in which individual accomplishment does not reign supreme. Here, the last shall be first, and those expecting reward will be turned away.

Jesus disarmed a stone-wielding mob by reminding the would-be throwers to consider their own shortcomings before attacking a woman accused of adultery (John 8:7).

This biblical witness reminds us that our lives are like Christ's — grounded in the love of God — so that we too might engage in acts of disarmament in the midst of our violent and angry world. Some youth in search of meaning and purpose in their lives will receive God's call to enact peaceful Christian practices. We hope they will find godparents, Sunday school teachers, and other faithful congregation members ready to walk alongside them in this path.

Seeking justice with compassion

Betsy Edwards, twenty-six, was expected to take a good position in her family's well-established printing company. Despite the lure of a lucrative career, Betsy followed a singular voice that, at a very early age, awakened her to the plight of the world's hungry. "From the second grade on," Betsy reflects "Mr. and Mrs. Jackson were part of my church, teaching me about the love of God and hunger awareness, always linked."

The Jacksons pour their volunteer energies into their United Methodist church's youth group. Led by them, Betsy went on summer gleaning trips to the Eastern Shore of Virginia and hunger awareness seminars in Washington, D.C. and engaged in year-round interpretation of these events back to the congregation through worship and education. After graduating from college, Betsy volunteered for a year through Lutheran Service Corps. She lived in intentional community, sharing household chores and a commitment to simple living. She worked with homeless and low-income seniors, lobbying to insure affordable units in a new development. This experience confirmed her desire to work in nonprofits, and she now has a job resourcing community groups as they support legislation directed at alleviating hunger in the state of California.

A local church — especially two adults within it — pointed Betsy toward the world's deep needs. Now her home congregation supports her from afar as she works out her emerging call. She draws on the deep well of Christian spirituality as she sees it reflected in the various denominations she encounters through her work in public advocacy. In a society that often measures success by the size of one's mortgage, Betsy has chosen a countercultural path, one directed toward compassion and justice.

The biblical record of Jesus' life and teachings contains numerous stories reflecting his heart of compassion for people and other living things. Neither the sparrow nor the blade of grass, neither the hair on one's head or the hemorrhaging woman goes unnoticed and uncared for in God's economy. God cares about individuals, and God works through the church community to manifest this care to the world. Betsy got this message through the example of a pair of committed Christians working out part of their vocations. They followed an incessant urge to immerse themselves in the struggle against hunger and poverty, discovering there a window to new truths.

•

During the summer of 2006, Englishman David Sharp died of oxygen depletion along a well-traveled route to the summit of Mount Everest. Dozens of people walked right past him, unwilling to risk their own ascents by stopping to save his life. At least one team did give him oxygen, but by then he was too near death to save. Wealthy, fit, extreme sports enthusiasts who had devoted lots of money and time in training were able to numb themselves to human suffering in pursuit of their goal.

Some thoughtful Christians see in this story a modern-day parable. Have we become so blinkered by our pursuit of our individual life's dreams and peak experiences that we can overlook the most basic human virtue of being a good neighbor to the one in need, as exemplified in the Gospel story of the Good Samaritan? (Luke 10:25–37).

What treasures — perhaps far greater than standing at the peak of Mount Everest — might have awaited those willing to change their plans, to redirect their energies and goals in order to help a fellow climber? What might happen if, instead of focusing solely on our own peak experiences, we travelers had in our possession a few trustworthy tenets reminding us of God's call of justice and service?

The tenets explored here — through the stories of young people who are *caring for the earth, exploring religious diversity,* practicing *peace making*, and following *compassion into paths of justice* — help us envision a church attuned to the whispers of the Holy, that presence who provides reliable hope in the face of multiple, competing, less-than-hopeful realities.

Finding trustworthy guides for emerging identities

Emerging from her three-day sickbed, Brenda found herself surrounded by women who confidently went about the work that was before them. On one level, that work had to do with baking ham and making potato salad. On another level, that work had to do with hands flying fast over fabric leaving intricate stitchwork and a warming quilt in their wake. Beneath these levels, though, there was other hard work, work that requires strengthening and sustaining. This kind of work pulls us out of our known pathways and calls us into places "where we did not plan to go." Such is the often costly work of Christian discipleship. Brenda's elders named the connection between their Christian faith and the very frightening challenge of integrating public places.

Brenda's elders were practicing what we might call a spiritual activism. It is a call to engage in certain Christian practices that will result in a changed world. Spiritual activism comes from taking seriously the hard questions of faith lived out in the world. It requires a new kind of training, a new curriculum, fostered and refined by a circle of Christians discerning God's call in their lives. It is a training very different from the training we receive through our culture, which primarily equips us to become good consumers. We can perform almost mindlessly the tasks of the marketplace and its cycles of desire, from which hardly any pockets of our lives remain untouched.[19] Habits of spiritual activism will take root only if we consistently remind ourselves of the church's role in the public sphere.

In this chapter, we have nosed around the stories of young people who are finding an alternative curriculum from which to carve out their vocational expressions. We have glimpsed the circles of care that support them. These circles provide an important psychological scaffolding that development theorists have long acknowledged as crucial for emerging identities.

James W. Fowler coined the much-quoted couplet "I see you seeing me: I see the you I think you see" to capture this experience of an adolescent constructing her emerging identity through the mirror provided by a trusted significant other.[20] This image helps explain the way young people develop their identity, not in isolation but in fluid, back-and-forth interaction with a community of peer and adult watchers. Young people imagine the way someone sees them, and often mirror back behaviors that do or do not fit the expectations. They watch for reactions and respond again in a sort of feedback loop.

When we apply this metaphor to congregational life, we see a church that helps youth imagine their lives as full of potential to heal a broken world. Is it not possible that a young person's vocation takes shape as caring adults reflect back what they see, imagine, or hope for in that younger one? Reciprocally, might not a congregation receive a new call, morphing (or developing, to use a more laden term) to the extent that it allows itself to be flexible in embracing a new generation's needs, desires, and responsiveness to the world?

---

19. Katherine Turpin, *Branded: Adolescents Converting from Consumer Faith* (Cleveland: Pilgrim Press, 2006).

20. James W. Fowler, *Stages of Faith: The Psychology of Human Development and the Quest for Meaning* (San Francisco: HarperCollins, 1995), 72.

If we adults watch emerging vocations of youth, bless those that bear the fruit of God, and join in actions to reverse the trends toward destruction, then we are indeed helping youth construct their identity as called ones capable of creating a more just, peaceful, and sustainable world. In return, the adult stakeholders in church will find their communities reshaped, perhaps not alarmingly or radically, but undeniably, as they respond lovingly to the good news God reveals through the young persons in their midst.

The next three chapters provide some practical ways to put these tenets into action within congregational life — during summer camping trips, on weekend excursions, at weeknight coffee-house gatherings, and in sleeping bags at the end of a day of a home-building mission. In Fowler's words, "Vocation derives from that profound sense that we are called into existence in this time and this place and among these people for the sake of investing our gifts and potentials in furthering some cause that is of transcending importance."[21] What better place than local congregations to test that hope?

---

21. James W. Fowler, *Faith Development and Pastoral Care* (Philadelphia: Fortress Press, 1987), 32.

Chapter 3

Nature as teacher

A small group of youth arrives at a protected wilderness area just before dawn. In silence they move singly or in pairs, fanning out across the varied terrain. One teen reaches a marsh after walking vigorously for an hour, and sits in meditative silence, listening to the sounds of insects, birds, and animals marking their existence in the world. Another youth strolls gradually along a wooded trail, stopping occasionally to write in her journal. Upon clearing the woods she breaks out into a gentle jog on the beach, concentrating on the music of waves and the ballet of brown pelicans in flight alongside her. In her mind she practices a form of centering prayer, repeating a phrase from Psalm 8: "Oh God, how majestic is your name in all the earth." Down the shore a few hundred yards, another pair of teens stumbles with anguished surprise upon a strangled sea gull caught in the plastic loops of discarded soft drink packaging.

The group continues in this pattern of contemplative immersion with nature, coming together after several hours. Over a communally prepared and shared meal, they reflect on their experiences and their encounters with plants, fish, birds, animals, water, wind, and soil. Several of these youth mention new awareness and insight about the creatures and ecology they have encountered. Some speak too of new insights about themselves in relation to the nonhuman creation. And many of them identify something about their encounter with nature that they relate to God — an awareness of the divine presence, a sense of awe in relation to creation, a feeling of inner calm or disturbance that they associate with the Holy as known in nature.

These youth and their adult leaders spend time strategizing about what they and their church can do to bring justice and promote the healing of creation, in light of their deepened sense of connection to nature and to God in nature. Actions such as intensifying the church's recycling efforts, educating others about the destructive impact of human garbage on fish and wildlife through a church fellowship program time, and personal commitments to lifestyle changes and political action are only some of the strategies named that day that will be lived out in the coming weeks and months.

For a few of the youth on the nature immersion that day, the length of time and human silence seemed nearly unbearable. "That's the longest I've been unplugged since I've been born!" one boy exclaimed. Another spoke about feeling "afraid out there," the unbounded space of the big sky and vast terrain opening up fears of being lost or "just getting absorbed — I'm so small and it's so big." For a few of the youth, the hours of human silence seemed too short. This temporary stilling of human and electronically produced noises allowed the hearing of new sounds and voices, those from animals, wind, insects, birds, and surf, that became a welcome cacophony in relief from the manufactured sounds filling their ears most other times.

These young people come from a small-town Episcopal congregation on the West Coast. Like other young people living in various urban, suburban, and small-town communities across the United States, these teens spend most of their day in "manufactured" settings, from high school hallways to plastic fast food restaurant seating. Parks, pathways, back yards, sports fields and other green spaces may provide brief moments of escape from artificial environments, but opportunities for deep immersions into nature do not happen often in the everyday lives of many young people today.

This chapter explores the power of an intentional engagement with nature in young peoples' processes of vocational discernment. We will consider the ways in which encounters with the natural world can constitute a core practice of youth ministry organized around inviting young people into Christian identity. So far in this book, we have been describing an alternative way of understanding and practicing youth ministry centered around vocation, or God's calling of young people to share their lives and gifts in God's broken-yet-beloved world. Our approach asserts that young people have lives to offer to a world crying out for healing, care, and reconciliation.

We have said that youth ministry should be about calling youth to their ministries, inviting and equipping them to take on their identities as Christians who live by offering themselves in the service of God's love and justice. In this approach, youth ministry becomes a companioned walk of youth and adults together who shape their lives and community around practices of faith. We use the language of "vocational discernment" to describe the processes by which young people explore and embrace a way of life situated in the practices of a faith community and shared with the world beyond it, through which these young people's "deepest desires meet the world's greatest needs."[1] In this chapter, we will explore intentional educational ministry with youth through encounters with nature as a means of fostering young people's journeys toward lives of care and justice.

Speaking of nature

The life of the planet is at stake. The earth and its creatures, particularly its nonhuman creatures, are in grave peril. Now-classic sources in the literature of ecological and environmental movements have addressed the causes and complexities of this situation in its religious dimensions.[2] These works cite in particular the problematic interpretations of the Genesis 1 creation story's call for humans to

---

1. Paraphrased, Frederick Buechner, *Wishful Thinking: A Seeker's ABC* (New York: Harper & Row, 1973), 95.
2. Lynn White, " The Historical Roots of Our Ecological Crisis," in *Readings in Ecology and Feminist Theology,* ed. M. H. MacKinnon and M. McIntyre (Kansas City, Mo.: Sheed and Ward, 1995), 25–35; Rosemary R. Ruether, "The Biblical Vision of the Ecological Crisis," *Readings in Ecology and Feminist Theology,* ed. M. H. MacKinnon and M. McIntyre (Kansas City, Mo.: Sheed and Ward, 1995), 75–81. See also Paul Santmire, "Ecology, Justice and Theology Beyond the Preliminary Skirmishes," *Readings in Ecology and Feminist Theology, Readings in Ecology and Feminist Theology,* ed. M. H. MacKinnon and M. McIntyre (Kansas City, Mo.: Sheed and Ward, 1995), 56–62.

"have dominion over" and "subdue" other creatures and the earth as a key religious rationale for human mistreatment of the nonhuman creation.[3] Other analysts note historical parallels between women and nature that justify the oppression of both.[4] Still other voices name the problem inherent in contemporary references to "nature" that romanticize it as if it were an object separated from history and culture, or similarly, as if humanity were not at all a part of nature.

In this chapter, we use the term "nature" broadly to refer to non-manufactured environments — the divine creation of seascapes, forests, wetlands, mountain ranges, and wilderness areas. We also use it in reference to urban green spaces that, while "manufactured" in the sense of being planned, shaped, and planted by people, exist because of the needs and desires of persons for connection with the nonhuman creation. Obviously human beings are a part of nature, but this often seems to be denied. In fact some of our ecological problems reflect the consequences of our treatment of the nonhuman biosphere as something in which humans do not participate and with which we do not identify ourselves. But for purposes of this chapter we will use the term "nature" primarily in reference to the nonhuman, non-manufactured elements of creation, in order to distinguish those from human beings and the products of human enterprise.

Environmental scientists and ecotheologians name two antithetical attitudes at the root of humanity's destructive treatment of the earth. On the one hand is the inability to recognize that we humans are a part of nature, such that its destruction is also our own demise.

---

3. M. A. Hinsdale, "Ecology, Feminism, and Theology," in *Readings in Ecology and Feminist Theology,* ed. M. H. MacKinnon and M. McIntyre (Kansas City, Mo.: Sheed and Ward, 1995), 196–207. Also Ruether, "The Biblical Vision of the Ecological Crisis," 75–81.

4. Carolyn Merchant, *The Death of Nature: Women, Ecology, and the Scientific Revolution* (New York: Harper & Row, 1990); see also Merchant, *Earthcare: Women and the Environment* (New York: Routledge, 1990), 141–45, for a brief synopsis of the convergence between feminism and environmentalism in the 1970s in the United States, and Sheri B. Ortner, "Is Female to Male as Nature Is to Culture?" *Readings in Ecology and Feminism,* ed. M. H. MacKinnon and M. McIntyre (Kansas City, Mo.: Sheed and Ward, 1995), 36–55.

On the other hand is the failure to distinguish between ourselves and creatures that are *not us*. This lack of distinction leads to an inability to recognize that the needs and interests of our species are not necessarily the same as those of other species or other parts of the creation. The first of these two attitudes invites an arrogant sense of superiority in which we humans view ourselves as "above nature," refusing to see our connection with it. The second of these attitudes invites harmful anthropocentrism or "human-centeredness." It is an attitude in which humans view all of reality from our own human-centered perspective, refusing to acknowledge the perspectives and integrity of others. In this view, nature exists merely to give us pleasure, to provide raw materials, and to serve as a backdrop for our endeavors. As Rosemary Ruether puts it, "In relation to humanity, nature no longer exists 'naturally,' for it has become part of the human social drama."[5] Ruether's comment points out that humans have colonized the rest of creation to such an extent that it is no longer possible for persons to even talk about nature legitimately without speaking of it in terms of human interests and concerns.

The developmental task most strongly associated with adolescence since Erik Erikson's foundational work is identity formation. This task concerns establishing a sense of one's own distinctiveness-in-relation to others. That is, adolescence is a time of developing a sense of one's own boundaries, or, as one youth put it, "recognizing where I stop and another (person or creature) begins." This sense of distinctiveness goes hand in hand with the parallel development of a sense of one's profound relatedness, of seeing one's self as a person in community with others (human and nonhuman). These parallel tasks of youth identity formation suggest adolescence as a prime moment to foster young people's awareness of their connection-in-difference not only with people but also with other parts of the creation. These realities make adolescence an optimal time for deep engagements in nature.

---

5. Ruether, "Biblical Vision of the Ecological Crisis," 75–81.

Connecting God, the environment, and vocation

Ask young people about times they feel closest to God and many will tell of an experience they have had in nature. "Whenever I'm in the woods or mountains, I feel God. I feel God when I'm with loving people at conferences and retreats also. But mostly I feel God when I'm alone in nature and thinking." These words are from Alisa, and she is not alone in voicing this sentiment that God may be known in nature in a particularly powerful way. An overwhelming number of the young people in our study of YTI youth answering a survey or interview question about times they experience closeness to God responded similarly.

Ask youth to reflect on where and how they experience a sense of awe at the wonder and grandeur of God, and again, many will speak of the nonhuman creation — the vastness of a sea's horizon, mountains stretching to the sky, the power and danger of a storm, or the surprising sound of an entire flock of geese landing in unison upon a lake. Ella described her sense of awe about God "when I look at a blue sky scattered with billowing clouds, so close, in fact that I identify blue and white as being holy colors. There are so many aspects about the sky that are absolutely mind-boggling that it makes me appreciate God's genius."

Whether on a stroll through a wooded city park, a camping trip, or a mountain hike with a church youth group, clearly one important context in which youth experience a connection with God is in nature. Cath, a young woman from a United Methodist congregation in the Midwest, echoed the language of the Genesis creation story when she described her connection to God through nature: "At camp there is a place called vesper hill. It overlooks a plush green valley. There is a simple wooden cross on the hill and beyond it you can see the whole valley. At sunset I feel close to God because I overlook the valley and think, 'This is Good.' "

Of course, not every young person has the kind of access to nature that cultivates the heightened awareness of the divine named by Ella or Cath. For some youth, economic realities mean there are few opportunities for significant encounters in nature: some youth cannot afford to go to camp or to travel outside the cities in which they live in order to be immersed in a nonhuman/natural environment. Others are "already immersed," living in rural environments but having few opportunities for reflective engagements with the religious dimensions of the nature surrounding them everyday. For other youth, social and cultural factors may limit their contact with nature. For example, if connections with nature are not valued and encouraged by family and community, then a young person may be less inclined to seek out opportunities to experience the natural world first hand. This restriction, like that of youth for whom the manufactured and virtual world of video games is preferable to direct experience in the out-of-doors, represents a constructed limitation that nevertheless results in limited access to nature.

We do not make the claim here that nature is the only (or even primary) place of encounter with the Holy for young people. Since God does not limit God's self-disclosure to the vehicle of nature alone, there are plenty of ways and means for young people to encounter God besides in the natural world. Here we simply note the fact that youth (and adults for that matter) tend to be "less wired" amid experiences in nature than at other times, and may have fewer distractions pressing upon them to divide their attention when immersed in the natural world, and so may create a space for experiencing God that gets crowded out in the busy-ness of everyday urban life. For whatever reason, it seems to be the case that among those youth having access to experiences with nature, there exists a strong relationship between nature and an experience of the presence of God.

Various theologians throughout the centuries have shared the perspective of these youth. John Calvin, for instance, called the creation "the mirror of divinity" and "the theatre of divine glory."[6] Centuries

---

6. John Calvin *Institutes of the Christian Religion,* ed. John T. McNeill, trans. Ford Lewis Battles, in collaboration with the editor and a committee of advisers (Philadelphia: Westminster Press 1960), I.5.1. See also Belden Lane, "Spirituality as the Performance of Desire: Calvin on the World as a Theatre of God's Glory," *Spiritus* 1, no. 1 (2001): 1–30.

before, Gregory Nazianzen imaged the creation and cosmos as the incarnation of prayer to God, with these words: "All that is, prays to you."[7] And contemporary theologian Sallie McFague refers to the world as "God's body."[8] Langdon Gilkey helpfully calls for Christians to reconstruct how humans value the nonhuman creation by extending the doctrine of *imago dei* to include other creatures.[9]

While countless Christians have understood nature as a special locus of divine revelation and a place for humans to encounter God, not all have understood their connection with the nonhuman biosphere as an aspect of Christian vocation. This seems like an especially peculiar gap in youth ministry, given the high value so many youth place upon nature's mediation of spirituality as exemplified in the above remarks of young people. This "disconnect" between seeing nature as spiritual, yet failing to see the human relationship with nature as part of a Christian call to ministry, shows up in a variety of approaches to nature commonly found in contemporary youth ministries.

Perspectives on nature

One approach involves young people in outdoor activities, but the out-of-doors functions as a staging ground or backdrop to recreational activities or high-impact emotional experiences that do not actually engage the youth in any significant sustained attention to nature itself. Some youth ministry programs, for example, advertise their annual ski trips with language that suggests a deep encounter with nature and God will occur through recreational activities like skiing or bungee jumping: "Experience God in nature: Ski Snow Mountain with the church youth group!" "Our God is an Awesome God — and you'll be sure of it when you go bungee jumping over Lake Tahoe!"

---

7. Attributed to Gregory Nazianzen.
8. Sallie McFague, *The Body of God: An Ecological Theology* (Minneapolis: Fortress, 1993).
9. Langdon Gilkey, *Nature, Reality, and the Sacred: The Nexus of Science and Religion* (Minneapolis: Fortress Press, 1993).

Young people may find their appreciation of God's creation or their sense of awe at God the Creator expanded by the exhilaration of these activities. But with the focus on the entertainment activity, and not on an encounter with the land, water, or creatures within that ecology, the relationship between youth and the earth remains one of a user to a resource or location. The point of the experience is recreation and exhilaration, and not an encounter with other creatures of God valued in and for themselves. Nature is scenery for the activity rather than integral to it.

A trip through the exhibit hall of Youth Specialties' National Youth Worker's Convention yields dozens of organizations marketing religious, nature-oriented youth trips. With names like "New Frontiers," "Confrontation Point," and "Noah's Ark Whitewater Rafting and Adventure Program," these organizations sell "ready-made adventure trips" for youth groups in which the thrill of extreme sports or high adventure outings such as kayaking and rock climbing becomes the vehicle through which they hope to encourage youth to a deeper faith. Some of the goals and values promoted by these organizations parallel those we see as central to practices of youth ministry concerned with vocation, justice, and the creation. These include:

- the educational value of nature immersion as a way to move young people out of their "comfort zones" toward inviting transformation;

- openness in young people that may be created by getting away from the distractions and interruptions of ever-present media such as music, video games, and cell phones;

- the potential for community building and for individual self-esteem enhancing activities set in an outdoor context that presents physical challenges to participants;

- the health-promoting features of physical activity involved in many of these nature-based experiences.

Taken in isolation from a wider concern of care for the earth, however, these goals and values have a rather exclusive focus on the human participants' immediate experience, apart from any attention on justice toward creation. The encounter with God in nature leads inward. Several of these organizations focus on individual religious awakening as the sole agenda of nature experiences. These programs give almost no attention to the need for action in everyday life to repair and heal the damages to earth wrought by destructive human patterns of living. There seems to be no awareness fostered about everyday life changes toward eco-justice that may flow from youth encounters with nature. These programs or nature-immersion experiences express an embedded understanding of religious education (and of Christian faith, for that matter) as exclusively concerned about the spiritual life (and salvation) of individual believers. Nature becomes reduced to a source for "object lessons" about God, and an object for use in personal spiritual experience. Indeed, fragile natural spaces might actually be endangered by these encounters in the form of wear and tear caused by high-impact trekkers.

Some programs of youth activity in the outdoors also have hidden political agendas that *actively* separate the encounter with God in nature from any concern for nature's well-being. Beyond simply not paying attention to matters such as human responsibility to protect old growth forests and endangered species, these groups wage an explicit campaign against making the connections between adoration of God in creation and eco-justice. An article from the non-denominational, evangelically oriented *Youthworker Journal* gives a tongue-in-cheek acknowledgement in a soft critique of this move:

> There can also be theological (and unfortunately political) reasons some of us may value nature less than we should. Sure our Bibles tell us that God created the cosmos (Genesis 1) and that nature reveals God's eternal power and divine nature (Romans 1). But isn't it the radical environmentalists (read: liberals) and pagans who hug trees and worship nature? Certainly good

Christian boys and girls wouldn't want to be found in such company![10] [parenthetical comments in original]

Like the T-shirt slogan by a conservative Christian hunting and gun promoting organization that reads, "Love the Creator, Not the Creation," conservative independent Christian organizations market wilderness trips as adventure experiences in which youth get to know God. The economics and politics of environmentalism are carefully kept away from the individualistic spirituality promoted there.

Even locally arranged retreats and church camp experiences may kindle in youth a false sense of having a deep encounter with nature, when in fact the encounter has been one of intense *communitas* with other persons. While the nonhuman creation does form an important part of the implicit curriculum of such camp experiences, without intentional efforts to foster direct encounter with the natural environment and its nonhuman plant and animal inhabitants, youth are unlikely to come away from these camps with a deep sense of compassion for other creatures and for the earth. They come away with a "high," a peak experience that they associate with nature because of the setting in which it happened. Beyond its role as staging ground, the earth and its nonhuman inhabitants have little actual significance within the experience. Learning *from* nature has no place in these experiences.

Karen-Marie Yust, a scholar in the field of Christian Education and Spirituality, makes a similar critique in her review of Christian camping programs. Attendees at these camps make an association between the intense emotional experience at the closing campfire, an encounter with God, and the nature-oriented location of the camp. But Yust critiques the kind of spirituality promoted by these experiences:

> Such experiences also suggest that spirituality is attached to emotion without reference to critical thinking, and that spirituality is about a mood or ambience rather than life practices.

---

10. Steve Rabey, "Saving Kids from 'Nature-Deficit Disorder,'" in *Youthworker Journal* (September–October 2005), accessed online at *www.youthspecialities.com/articles/topics/cultural/naturedd.php?*. Access date 10/30/2005.

They imply that one must obtain spirituality from special places that have it, rather than seeking God wherever one is. Whatever genuine elements of encounter with God may be present in the typical camp "mountaintop experience," the context can obscure the possibility of relating to God in the midst of ordinary activities and ordinary relationships.[11]

Experiences of sustained engagement with nature among youth, like the contemplative immersion experience described at the opening of this chapter, are efforts to bring intentionality to the religious dimensions of youth encounters with the natural world. Such encounters need not be merely romantic notions of divinity directly experienced in nature with no concern for social justice. Instead of simply assuming that God will be "found" in God's creation by youth who move into the out-of-doors, this kind of experience involves youth in preparation for encounters with nature and the Holy through learning and selecting various contemplative practices, and through engaging in activist practices. Lectio divina, examen, centering prayer, intercessory prayer, silent contemplation, journaling, and various forms of body prayer all are resources from Christian tradition that youth practice along with their adult companions. Through this emphasis on contemplative practices and the strategy session imagining actions in solidarity with the earth, their experience of God through nature immersion becomes "portable." That is, when youth engage in practices of faith in nature that they also can practice in other contexts of their everyday lives, their experience of the Holy is not restricted to a "mountaintop location" (although it certainly can take on particular and special significance there).

Another approach to nature found in some youth ministries assumes an automatic character-building capacity to any experiences youth have in nature. This viewpoint sometimes can be found hand-in-hand with a romantic idea that encounters with nature automatically operate to cure persons of the supposed corruption that

---

11. Karen-Marie Yust, "Creating an Idyllic World for Children's Spiritual Formation," *International Journal of Children's Spirituality* 11, no. 1 (2006): 182.

comes from urban living. These perspectives are prominent in church ministries with youth where the rhetoric of offering wholesome alternatives to the (ostensibly unhealthy or morally questionable) activities of contemporary youth culture constitutes the primary rationale for doing youth ministry.[12]

Youth ministry activities that take place in the out-of-doors involving some kind of physical challenge (such as high ropes courses, or scaled-down wilderness survival experiences modeled on programs like Outward Bound) may foster individuals' self-esteem, or develop a sense of group identity and cohesion, all in the context of an outdoor environment. Yet in these activities the focus still remains on the human participants and their experiences, for which nature is a setting. The "otherness" of the nonhuman creatures there, and a respectful and direct engagement with them, is not part of the explicit teaching. In fact, the treatment of nature as location for human-oriented adventures has the implicit effect of turning nature into a commodity for human use, with little inherent value of its own.

We are not suggesting here that there is anything necessarily wrong with recreational activities, camping trips, the building of group cohesion and communitas, or the encouragement of individual self-esteem, as a part of youth ministry. Nor do we mean that these types of activities are automatically incompatible with deep engagement with the natural world. These activities may well participate in the larger framework of a young person's experience in nature that shape dispositions of connection and care for the earth. For both of us, our own childhood and youth experiences with camping, retreats, and

---

12. These character-building and anti-urban approaches to nature also occur in youth-serving organizations outside the churches. For example, one of the key assumptions out of which Robert Baden-Powell founded boy scouting was the idea that military service in wartime built character among young men, but in times of peace, experiences in nature could accomplish a similar goal. See Jay Mechling, *On My Honor: Boy Scouts and the Making of American Youth* (Chicago: University of Chicago Press, 2001), 126, 260; see also Michael Rosenthal, *The Character Factory: Baden-Powell and the Origins of the Boy Scout Movement* (New York: Pantheon Books, 1986). I appreciate the comments of Chris Rodkey bringing this scouting connection to my attention.

outdoor recreation certainly testify to the power of such events to help orient persons toward a love of nature. We are not arguing against these experiences *per se.*[13]

Rather, our critique is this: in the absence of any intentional practices that involve youth in a focused experience with nature, these kinds of activities maintain human beings at the center of the experience. They do not necessarily foster deeper knowledge, compassion, respect, or care for the creation. But, problematically, these activities may give the appearance of being a significant encounter with the earth just because they get young people "out in nature." Such activities thus easily take the place of more substantive engagements with the earth, substituting for a different kind of experience in which nonhuman creatures as *others* in their own rights are as important in the encounter as is the human experience of it.

Finally, there is a problematic assumption about nature itself underlying some existing youth ministry approaches to nonhuman environments, best described as a tendency to romanticize nature. It is true that "awe and wonder" are common responses to the encounter with nature by young people who may well associate these with the power and splendor of God. But nature is not only and always awe-inspiring, nor are its processes necessarily beneficent. On December 27, 2004, a powerful tsunami brought death and destruction to thousands of people and other creatures in Asian countries. And even as we write this, the devastating effects continue from multiple hurricanes on U.S. communities in the Gulf States. These destructive events are part of nature too. The image of a coyote ripping apart the muscles of the rabbit it catches for food is not beautiful or benevolent. But it too is nature.

An alternative approach to engaging nature in youth ministry is needed, one that can:

---

13. Jessica Kovan and John Dirkx describe the impact of such experiences in the lives of committed environmentalists: in " 'Being Called Awake': The Role of Transformative Learning in the Lives of Environmental Activists," *Adult Education Quarterly* (February 2003): 99–118.

- "love the Creator *and* the creation," inviting youth into practices of responsibility, respect, and restoration with the earth in their everyday lives as part of Christian vocation;
- engage nature as a Subject with inherent value apart from utility for human consumption or enjoyment;
- learn *from* nature;
- balance critical thinking and interpretation of religious experiences connected to nature with elements of mystery and "unmediated" experience that also may be part of such encounters;
- help youth locate themselves in earth's ecosystem, as creatures both interrelated with, and distinct from, the others of the earth;
- resource the experiential religious encounters of youth in nature with critical reflection through the rich and varied theological and biblical resources for reflection on God and creation; and
- feed back into the corporate life of the larger faith community.

The example of contemplative nature immersion with which this chapter began is but one of many ways of engaging youth in nature as part of the quest for Christian vocation. We detail other examples below. What we are describing cannot be "programmed" in a single activity. It is, instead, part of an overall orientation within youth ministry of the Christian vocation of ministry with the earth.

Supporting youth vocations of solidarity with the earth in a consumer society

In the context of North American consumer culture and a mentality shaped by market forces it is easy for the concept of vocation to be collapsed into the market notion of privatized career choice. Earlier in this book we expressed an understanding of vocation that goes against some views of it as a matter of individual, private choice. While people do exercise agency, there is also an important sense in which vocation as a calling comes from outside of us and is not generated completely by us. There is always a public quality to vocation.

There is also an important theological element of Christian vocation that concerns God as the One Who Calls. The public character of vocation may be seen in the ways in which communities ratify or put their seal of approval on a person's response to a divine call. But a significant shadow side to the public character of vocation is that multiple communities and publics attempt to exercise their claims on the lives of youth, with market forces being a particularly powerful shaper of identity and vocation.

In our interviews with youth at YTI, we found many young people who articulated sophisticated understandings of vocation's public quality even as they talked about that aspect of vocation concerning their future work. In several instances, however, these young people pointed out tensions between the "calling" of market forces in North American consumer culture and an alternative faith-based call to offer their lives, skills, and passions in meaningful ways not necessarily rewarded by money or status.

Amy, for example, is a young person with an explicit set of theological criteria for defining her vocation: a calling should combine what one enjoys doing with what is most needed and meaningful. Amy believes that she is "meant to be" an organic farmer, someone who cultivates the earth in responsible and sustainable ways to provide for people's needs for good food. When asked about her current sense of what she is called to do and be with her life, at seventeen years Amy responded, "I think what I would really like to do is farming. . . . [I am gaining] a sense of responsibility toward the earth. And that's what made me want to be an organic, sustainable kind of farmer. Also it's something that everybody needs. . . . Also, I like to work with my hands as well as my brain. So it seems to fit into a lot of the different things that I'm interested in, which are practical and enjoyable and meaningful."

Amy worries about her ability to stay focused on this vocational path. "There's probably tons of things that would be good for me to do, but I just hope that if it does change it still fits that criterion of 'does it help someone' or 'does it fit with what I value?' . . . [There are also] barriers to being a farmer — I think land is expensive. I don't have a lot of experience. A lot of people laugh at me when I say I want to be a farmer, and I'm like, 'Okay.' So there's not a lot of support in general. If I tell people I'm interested in medicine, they say, 'Wow, you know, both your parents are doctors, it would be great' — but it's not the same kind of social pride in having a farmer in your family." She is critical of American cultural notions of "the good life" shaped around "impressing others, being looked at by other people who say, 'Wow, they have a successful life.'"

Amy credits some of her teachers, and the opportunity to participate in a special program of environmental education, with shaping her vocational commitments to the earth. At the Friends' (Quaker) school she attends, Amy encountered an educational philosophy and practice grounded in "the connectedness of people within a school community, and wider and wider communities."

A practice of youth ministry constituted around Christian vocation would support Amy's present-day actions to be in solidarity with the earth through gardening and other activities. It would offer her opportunities, biblical and theological resources, and a community with whom to reflect on the links between the foods humans grow and consume, and Christian moral imagination. And it would be a place of opportunity for action and service in relation to her faith, supporting her present-tense vocation and funding its future adult incarnations with care.

Nature as teacher

What educational perspectives can ground and support ministry with youth that equips them for Christian vocation both now in adolescence and later in their adult lives? Two writers are particularly helpful. One is C. A. Bowers, an educational theorist concerned about creating "education for an ecologically sustainable culture." Bowers contends that a major barrier to ecologically sound education is the way our society defines intelligence. An individually centered view of intelligence, he asserts, problematically represents individuals as the primary social units, and associates intelligence with processes occurring in the brain or mind of an individual.[14] Consequently, the criteria for viewing a thought or action as intelligent relate to the individual, regardless of its consequences on the rest of the human and nonhuman community. For example design for a nuclear bomb is considered brilliant because of the intricate cognitive processes involved in its development, regardless of its world-damaging and destructive capacities.

In contrast, Bowers argues for a view of intelligence that locates it in the culture at large rather than exclusively within individual minds. In doing so, Bowers articulates a perspective on what intelligence consists of that "takes account of the problem of living in a sustainable relationship with the rest of the biotic community"[15] as its central issue. Things are measured as intelligent, then, when they meet the criterion of contributing to sustainability.

Bowers moves against the major traffic flow in contemporary educational theory, with its emphasis on learners as knowledge constructors who develop their own meaning systems. He contends that such a perspective makes the learners' "own experiences the primary reference point for evaluating what knowledge and which values will have primary authority in their lives."[16] Bowers contends instead that sustainability and cultural continuity depend upon the ability of one generation to communicate and teach its best wisdom and values to a new generation. Continuity concerns "the ability [of people] to live in relative balance with the ecosystems they are dependent upon. That is, no culture that has met the challenge of long-term sustainability carried on its primary educational processes by instilling in its young a bias against the knowledge of the older generation."[17]

Recognizing the possible misunderstanding of his idea as a kind of nostalgic romanticism, Bowers acknowledges that the older generation

---

14. C. A. Bowers, *Educating for an Ecologically Sustainable Culture: Rethinking Moral Education, Creativity, Intelligence, and Other Modern Orthodoxies* (Albany: State University of New York Press, 1995), 106.
15. Ibid., 113.
16. Ibid., 15.
17. Ibid., 17.

may also capitulate to the individualistic values of consumerism. It is therefore important to distinguish between "olders" and "elders" in the community. The latter are those who bear and communicate the community-enhancing values and practices that can sustain the larger ecosystem of which the community is a part. In short, Bowers asserts that long-term survival "depends in part on our collective ability to accumulate, communicate, and renew ecologically sustainable forms of knowledge and values."[18] Such abilities make "transgenerational communication" imperative (a perspective he names as a distinct alternative to the current educational emphasis on student-centered learning). They require a "shift from youth oriented culture to one that shares some characteristics of more traditional and ecologically-centered cultures,"[19] meaning that the elders of the culture must be recognized as carriers of essential knowledge and values.

In these assertions, Bowers's perspective may seem odd in a contemporary book on youth ministry and vocation. But what he offers with them is critical to the perspective on youth ministry as a companioned walk of young people with adults in the practices of Christian ministry. First, he emphasizes the well-being of the whole creation as the norm against which intelligence and education are measured. In the framework for youth engagements with nature that we have been describing, good Christian education and intelligent youth ministry cannot simply attend to what happens for youth. It must also contribute to the rest of the created order. Second, Bowers contends that there are normative values and claims in cultural traditions that can guide present-day practices. Bowers refers, of course, to cultural rather than religious traditions. But his point underscores the significance in faith communities of valuing the received heritage — the stories and narratives of scripture, theological arguments, historical experience — of our theological traditions. Third, Bowers names interaction between the generations as crucial. In a vision of youth

---

18. Ibid., 135.
19. Ibid.

ministry where seasoned practitioners of Christian faith help to apprentice others in those practices constitutive of Christian identity, the engaged and active presence of several generations of adults with youth is imperative.

Mary Elizabeth Moore is a second scholar whose work helps to frame our vision of youth ministry. The practices of youth ministry described above have a communal and public quality to them. That is, in youth ministry organized around assisting youth to shape a vocation through practices in Christian community that can matter for the world, the point of profound engagement with nature is not merely what happens for the youth (although that is important). The point of such engagements must also concern what happens with and for the world. A theologian and religious educator, Moore frames this matter well in her description of human involvements with the creation as a "sacred vocation." In her book *Ministering with the Earth*, Moore recalls the familiar Genesis creation story in which God speaks the world into existence. In this biblical creation account, the words "In the beginning . . . " set in motion the narrative of God's action to create a world of seas and land, filled with plants and animals of great diversity. Human beings are a part of the creation story, and in that story God gives to them responsibility of caring for the earth. Moore evokes this biblical story as she contends that it is time for human beings today to make a *new beginning* in ministry with the earth. Making a new beginning is part of our "sacred vocation of ministry with the earth."[20]

Moore's understanding of sacred vocation, like the focus on vocation framing this entire volume, is a theological one carrying with it the claim that how we use our lives matters to God. She names three particular actions needed for humanity's sacred vocation of ministry with the earth: "*compassion,* or feeling with God and creation; *reflection* on God and the world and the relationship between them;

---

20. Mary Elizabeth Moore, *Ministering with the Earth* (St. Louis: Chalice Press, 1998), 145.

and *active participation* in reshaping community, social, and environmental life."[21] These three actions also comprise three movements in a practice of education with youth where nature is teacher. Such education might take shape through:

- Various activities designed to engender a sense of compassion for the creation through identification with other creatures and by cultivating greater knowledge of the peril and destruction faced by so much of the nonhuman biosphere. One educator uses documentary films to raise consciousness and compassion for the plight of animals whose habitats are disappearing.[22] Another creates "alternative tours" from an animal's or bird's imagined perspective of places such as fast food restaurants or manufacturing centers that look at an area of human activity in terms of its impact on others creatures.[23] Such educational activities invite youth to empathy and compassion with the earth.

- Opportunities for discussion, reading, study, and worship that engage in critical reflection on God, God's creation, and the relation between them. A pastor in Sunnyvale, California, regularly combines wilderness trips for intergenerational groups in his congregation with classes to study theology and scripture focused on his Reformed tradition's understanding of the doctrine of creation.[24] Others include nonhuman creatures and the environment in prayers of intercession and in preaching.

---

21. Ibid.
22. Robert Figueroa, "Teaching for Transformation: Lessons from Environmental Justice," in *The Environmental Justice Reader: Politics, Poetics and Pedagogy,* ed. Joni Adamson, Mei Mei Evans, and Rachel Stein (Tucson: University of Arizona Press, 2002), 311–30.
23. "A Seagull Visits McDonalds," unpublished curriculum for youth by Joyce Ann Mercer, Hartford, Conn., 1983, Center City Church's Center for Youth and Community Resources.
24. A central part of the ministry of Pastor Steve Harrington is his leadership of various nature-based experiences, from kayaking and backpacking to camping and day hikes. Harrington wrote a D.Min. dissertation project on outdoor and wilderness ministry. Steve Harrington, "Developing a Biblical and Theological Foundation for Christian Wilderness Adventure Ministries," D.Min. Advanced Pastoral Studies Program. San Anselmo, California, San Francisco Theological Seminary, 1998, 300.

- Active participation in a congregation's everyday practices of waste disposal to incorporate "green policies" in everything from the installation of low-flush toilets to the purchasing of office supplies. Other actions might include mission trips organized around partnership with communities experiencing eco-racism, in which racial and ethnic minorities and the poor disproportionately bear the burdens of destructive consumption and waste generation by others. Youth can participate in influencing environmental policies in their schools, and in their governments through joining with others to lobby for legislative change.

Seeing God's fingerprints

"The heavens are telling the glory of God, and the firmament [earth] proclaims God's handiwork" (Ps. 19:1), sang the psalmist in the Hebrew Bible centuries ago. New versions of this ancient song are still sung by people today. Hank, a seventeen-year-old high school student at YTI with aspirations of becoming an environmental lawyer, offered his version of the psalmist's incantation with these words: "[Other people] disconnect from the tangible evidence of God and then complain, 'There is no proof.' Look to nature and you can see God's fingerprints on life itself." Across the ages, then, human beings have looked to their encounters with the nonhuman creation, perceiving there the presence and work of God. Will our youth ministries call young people now and in the future to vocations of Christian life in which they participate in practices of justice and solidarity with creation?

Nature and contemplative listening

In this chapter we have explored the power of immersion in the nonhuman natural world to foster the vocational journeys of young people. In chapter 4, we turn to another kind of immersion: immersion in in-depth conversational encounters between youth and adults, which we term "holy listening." In a world where technology often substitutes for face-to-face contact, youth and adults alike rarely experience a calm, welcoming other who seems to have "all the time in the world" to listen. We imagine the work of youth ministry as such contemplative listening. Adults accompanying young people in their walks of faith may create listening spaces where the meaning of life is invited to unfold.

Chapter 4

Holy listening

Only in one's mother tongue can one express one's own truth.
In a foreign language the poet dies.[1]

In a collection called *The Book of Questions*, Chilean poet Pablo Neruda asks "Whom can I ask what I came to make happen in this world?" I, Dori, first encountered this line in 1993 while preparing to take a group of North American youth to the Atacama Desert in Chile for their first international mission trip. Emily, then sixteen, grasped this line and refused to let it go. It became our oft-whispered mantra. Someone would utter it as we gazed at the stars after a day spent playing soccer with barefoot children, as we hammered assembly-line fashion the desks and chairs that would furnish their school, or as we strolled through the dusty cemetery surrounded by the majestic Andes mountains.

Neruda's question is a shorthand articulation of the profound developmental task of discerning vocation.[2] The journey outside our everyday lives — to a foreign landscape, awash in an unfamiliar language, and encircled by new friends — invited us to evoke one another's truths about life's big questions.

Now twenty-seven, Emily spends her summers slogging through the wetlands of Wisconsin, collecting and interpreting dirt samples.

---

1. Paul Celan, *Gesammelte Werke,* Frankfurt am Main, as quoted in Shoshana Feldman and Dori Laub, *Testimony: Crises of Witnessing in Literature, Psychoanalysis, and History* (New York: Routledge, 1992).

2. See Sharon Daloz Parks, *Big Questions, Worthy Dreams: Mentoring Young Adults in Their Search for Meaning, Purpose, and Faith* (San Francisco: Jossey-Bass, 2000), for a discussion of discerning vocation as a life-long task that is particularly acute during adolescence and young adulthood.

She is an environmental scientist dedicated to diminishing the impact of development on the mating grounds of the region's endangered species. As a pastoral presence who watched from a distance as this particular expression of vocation unfolded, I celebrate that Emily found "meaningful work consistent with her faith and values."[3] For help in deciphering her vocational urges, Emily turned to her peers, her parents, her youth group, and her particularly attuned biology teacher. With humor, angst, and many late-night conversations, Emily solicited the help of others to clarify the inner voice leading toward "what she came to make happen in this world."

- Where do people engage in deep listening to the emerging longings of teens?

- Who is taking the time to immerse youth in cross-cultural experiences and then tease out their impact on emerging beliefs?

- When are youth invited to slow down, take a look around, and tell the truth of their lives out loud to one another?

Hopefully, this happens in the course of any good ministry by, with, and for youth. But as watchers and practitioners of youth ministry well know, carving out space and time for deep reflection is challenging. In the influential book *Practicing Our Faith* and its companion for youth, *Way to Live,* the authors invite exploration of the ancient Christian practice of testimony, defined as the act of telling the truth of our lives out loud to one another.[4] But inviting youth to "testify" can feel forced and unnatural. The word "testimony" connotes the recital of a conversion experience rather than honest talk about God's activity in the daily events of the here-and-now.

---

3. Margaret Ann Crain and Jack Seymour, *Yearning for God: Reflections of Faithful Lives* (Nashville: Upper Room Books, 2003), 47.

4. Dorothy C. Bass, ed., *Practicing Our Faith: A Way of Life for a Searching People* (San Francisco: Jossey-Bass, 1997), and Don Richter and Dorothy C. Bass, *Way to Live: Christian Practices for Teens* (Nashville: Upper Room Books, 2002).

We want to widen the definition of testimony, allowing it to include emerging stories that give meaning to one's life.[5] In this view, testimony refers not only to reporting on God's already-finished activity in the world, but also includes the voicing of memories of an experience, event, or relationship that has been tucked into the seams of everyday living. When invited, these stories might pour forth and come into focus as significant testimony to God's activity in the small moments of life. In the presence of an artful listener, a youth may better be able to discern a pattern of calling, claiming, and ongoing revelation woven through these life events.

We have witnessed the consistent creation of space and time in which authentic testimony such as this is evoked in young people. Amazingly, it happens quite regularly as the by-product of a purportedly more significant goal, the gathering of academic research on the spiritual lives of teens. Research with adolescents using semiformal, open-ended, one-on-one interviews exemplifies the creation of testimonial space. The interview itself provides both a generative metaphor and a practical guide for the wider practice of youth ministry.

The interview: Holy listening to inchoate testimony

The interviews to which we refer took place at the Youth Theological Institute (YTI), a four-week program for high school seniors at Candler School of Theology on the campus of Emory University. Embedded in the YTI experience over the past eleven years has been an extensive one-on-one interview with each participant.

We turned to these interviews expecting to analyze the content of adolescent movement toward vocational calling. Midstream, we redirected our gaze because we saw something rare and beautiful occurring: youth giving voice to their deepest longings.

---

5. For more on practices of religious education that evoke testimony, see Dori Grinenko Baker, *Doing Girlfriend Theology: God-Talk with Young Women* (Cleveland: Pilgrim Press, 2005).

In the midst of these interviews, the speaker often pauses, settles into a rhythm, and begins to divulge fresh truths. With only the briefest of prompts from the listener, the speaker sorts out the possibility of a fulfilling future, sometimes one that is radically countercultural. The speaker makes urgent use of this rare audience, basking in the undivided attention of a listening "other" to test significant new meanings.[6]

Might this rare moment — achieved while looking for something else — deserve sharing with a wider audience? We propose that the structure of the one-on-one, adult-youth interview might provide a unique invitation into exactly the type of deep sharing young people need and faith communities are uniquely prepared to offer.

To keep this startling, grace-filled moment within the confines of academic research would be akin to keeping quiet the serendipitous discovery of a particularly slippery substance called Teflon, whose potential usefulness redirected the gaze of researchers looking for better refrigerants. A similar happy accident resulted in the discovery of a reusable adhesive now ubiquitous in the form of Post-Its. With these two examples in mind, we widened our gaze to look beyond the content of the interview to the process itself. As we take a close look at one youth-adult interview that exemplifies the process of holy listening, we will harvest clues for those who wish to evoke radically fresh testimony from the youth in their midst.

Cara: Three testimonies unfold

Cara is a seventeen-year-old Hispanic girl who lives in rural Georgia.[7] She is nearing the end of her month-long stay at YTI. She is interviewed by Mary, a YTI staff member and graduate student.

---

6. Researchers and designers of YTI's interview tool came to understand that the interview functioned as a de facto part of the curriculum, becoming an educational intervention, despite the fact that it was not intended as such. See Joyce Ann Mercer, *GirlTalk on Faith and Families* (San Francisco: Jossey-Bass, forthcoming).

7. The names of both interviewer and interviewee have been changed to protect their identities.

Mary sets the framework for the interview by introducing three broad questions:

1. How would you describe the family, church, and community in which you were formed?

2. What kind of ideas or experiences have you had as an adolescent that have destabilized or called into question your early faith?

3. What resources, practices, or ideas are you finding helpful as you put the pieces of faith together again?

Written into these questions are assumptions about the adolescent and young adult years as a crucial time of identity formation during which religious ideals become tested, reconfigured, and finally claimed as one's own. In this type of semi-structured interview, the interviewer follows a predetermined guide of open-ended questions. The questions are designed not so much for the presentation of knowledge already acquired, but to provide a site for the construction of self-knowledge.[8]

At the start of the interview, Cara's responses are brief and somewhat clipped. The listener provides questions that help Cara give an autobiographical account of her childhood years. As she moves deeper into the interview, Cara's answers grow longer and the interviewer retreats into the background, allowing Cara to lead. In answer to the question "What are the values you think you have deeply internalized? What are the things that are important to you?" Cara begins the first of stories we classify as emerging "testimonies." These are moments when she tells the truth of her life out loud to a listener, finding within the stories traces of God's activity in her life-world.

The first testimony is a lengthy reflection on Cara's grandmother, who travels to the United States from Latin America each year to visit her adult children and their families. The visit has just recently ended, and Cara notes an interesting phenomenon. All the money given to

---

8. For more on the epistemology of the interview, see Steinar Kvale, *InterViews: An Introduction to Qualitative Research Interviewing* (Thousand Oaks, Calif., and London: Sage, 1996).

her grandmother by comparatively wealthy North American relatives for the purchase of "necessities" is funneled back to relatives, friends, and associates in her home country. "I mean it's ridiculous," Cara states as she reflects on this flow of money through her grandmother's hands. "She doesn't even know the person, and she'll buy something for them. She just knows someone that knows them. She just gives non-stop, and she will not buy herself anything. It's kind of ridiculous because, you're like, there's essentials and stuff like that. But in her mind, it's not ridiculous, it's essential to always give."

As Cara continues to reflect on what is "essential" in her grand-mother's life, she both critiques and admires this self-less giving. She reflects on her grandmother's lifetime of activity as a seemingly traditional wife and mother who pours time and energy into her church and community, managing to raise enough funds to save an orphanage. Cara ends this testimony by stating "If I was like half the person she is, I would definitely have achieved my goal as a person, you know."

In the second testimony, Cara reflects upon being discriminated against because of her Hispanic heritage. Until moving to a rural area, Cara had always thought of racial discrimination as something that happened to African Americans. "That was my mentality," she says. "I was shocked that there was discrimination toward Hispanics." She describes how the dawning realization of her status as a minority "makes my life difficult, because it really just makes me want to move."

She shares how this experience affected her faith. "My faith kind of dwindled when I was experiencing this because I was kind of mad at God, you know? Like, why are you letting this happen to me?" Cara's parents, whom she described as trusted companions in past life-crises, were not helpful resources to her in this instance, because they had been raised in a very different cultural milieu. She describes looking outside her family of origin for help and finding it in a friendship with an African American girl. This friendship became the resource to help her move through her shock, anger, and eventual integration of the experience.

Through the course of describing the discrimination and the way she dealt with it, Cara makes sense of the experience as an opportunity for her to embrace her heritage and remember the pride of her ancestry. "I was always proud, you know, but now I have more pride in who I am." During portions of this testimony, Cara hesitates in articulating her feelings. The listener quietly interjects helping prompts such as "yeah, I agree" and "I'm sure."

The third testimony appears as the interview is nearing a close. When Mary asks, "Are there other things, besides, you know, the prejudice you've experienced, that have been jarring for you?" Cara tells about the death of a close friend named John. The story unfolds without any interruption, as if it has been waiting to pour forth and is finally allowed to flood the now-intimate space between the Cara and the listener.

She expresses a profound sadness in the wake of his death. "I became depressed for many months... I didn't turn away from God completely, but it was kind of like I wondered why. I wanted my questions answered." She tells about her friendship with John, whom she'd known for several years. As a result of his mother's persistence, Cara had invited him to church events:

> I used to call him every single Sunday for months. Are you going to youth group, John? And he'd be like, "No, I'm going to stay here and watch T.V." And it's through that kind of persistent annoying him that... he actually did begin to come. And he attended regularly up until his death. And after he died, it was kind of like there was this kind of thankfulness from his mom toward me.... I think, I mean, it's just God working through you.... It was just, kind of, a thing that I do.

Throughout this interview, Cara is led into a place of safety in which to tell the truth of her life out loud to a listening other. As she talks about her grandmother, she identifies a longing to emulate her ethic of giving. As she talks about experiencing discrimination, she recovers latent pride in her heritage and claims the decision to live into it more fully. As she makes sense of the loss of a close friend,

she claims the significance of the role she played in his life and voices
the belief that her everyday act was used by God in a redemptive
way. Cara voices three significant life experiences and moves toward
integrating them with her emerging sense of purpose. Through the
interview, Cara names pieces of her vocational call, portions of the
puzzle of "what she came to make happen in this world," not only
in some distant future, but also in her current existence.

Harvesting clues: The interviewer's role in evoking testimony

Throughout this interview and others conducted as part of YTI, the
interviewer does not pretend to be a removed, unbiased researcher.
At times, exchanges between the two parties reflect a recent common
experience in worship, a class, or a community-wide conversation.
The youth-adult relationship reflected in the interviews ranges from
at best a close association as mentor or teacher to, at the very least, a
witnessing bystander. During the weeks leading up to the interview,
the youth has formed new relationships, learned to open scripture in
different ways, negotiated conflict between individuals and groups,
and been exposed to the intersection of faith and public life through
such issues such as racism, heterosexism, and global justice. The
adult interviewers were also immersed in this community as mentors,
guides, and small group leaders.

The interviewer uses her privileged position as a part of a particularly challenging and growth-inducing milieu to make a certain
level of disclosure possible in the speaker. It is as if the adult's presence in the ecology of the community fosters a climate of trust in
which authentic testimony to life experience is primed to take place.
In this time set apart, the interviewer focuses on the individual. As
the rhythm of the interview is established, the speaker settles into the
luxury of having found a "holy listener."

The position of the listener in these interviews is similar to that of
a youth minister, pastor, or adult volunteer who has accompanied a

youth during a life-changing experience, be it an overseas mission trip or the loss of a friend or loved one. A watcher, participant, witness, and guide, the youth minister stands uniquely positioned to create a space for critical reflection on such experiences. Those who walk alongside youth in faith communities might seize particular moments such as these to invite the youth to be "interviewed." The purpose of the interview is not to help a needy youth, but to provide space for theological integration of significant life events. A by-product is to inform an interested adult and perhaps a wider faith community about one significant journey with God that is currently underway.[9] This seemingly subtle shift in focus creates an audience in which authentic testimony might occur.

It is important to acknowledge that there exists a power differential between the interviewer and the interviewee, similar to that which always exists between youth and adults who work with them. Many youth will feel obligated to submit to an interview when asked by an adult. Therefore, adults must be extremely careful to make clear that the interview is purely voluntary and that any youth who chooses to decline the offer might do so without any embarrassment. Furthermore, the adult who conducts the interview must be clear about its purposes. For instance, it would not be appropriate for an adult to use as a sermon illustration anything that arose during an interview without the express permission of the interviewee.

A Proposal for youth ministry: Creating an ethos of holy listening

The interview Cara experienced opened a profound moment of holy listening and authentic testimony. In the everyday lives of teenagers, this level of listening is most likely to occur in professional therapy or

---

9. In interviewing youth for academic research, adults must obtain signed consent forms from the youth and their parents. The researcher commonly agrees to withhold the name of the interviewee in any sharing of the collected data. I suggest youth ministers who engage in interviewing youth might adopt the same practice. For more on the ethical considerations involved in interviewing, see Kvale, *InterViews*.

counseling sessions. Unfortunately, most of today's youth will only make it to such spaces as a result of pathological behavior. Boys who "act out" through the use of drugs, alcohol, or violence may be referred or mandated to undergo counseling. Girls who "act in" through depression, suicide attempts, or cutting may find their way to helpful counseling.[10] The expense of such professional treatment makes it a scarce commodity. Moreover, the counseling often focuses on the acute needs of the youth, leaving little time for larger issues of purpose and meaning-making to surface. In short, "There appear to be few places left where persons can experience themselves being listened to with deep attention for two entire hours," wrote Joyce, when reflecting on these interviews, some of which she designed for YTI and used while completing her dissertation at Emory University. "Not even psychotherapy offers that! Using research interviews as a framework for a conversation about life and faith invites youth to narrate their life stories in terms of the people, events, and ideas shaping their worlds — and to be listened to by another person."[11]

The church would provide a great service to youth in contemporary U.S. culture if it created a climate where this type of holy listening is fostered regularly, not as a cure for lives gone astray, but as an aid for healthy development.

Over the past ten years, we authors have each engaged in ethnographic listening to girls and women in small groups within congregations, neighborhoods, and friendship circles. Encouraged by the richness of these ethnographic encounters and similar experiences reported by others who have adapted the methods of qualitative research to the field of congregational studies, we began incorporating interview assignments into our introductory courses on youth

---

10. See Mary Pipher, *Reviving Ophelia: Saving the Selves of Adolescent Girls* (New York: Ballantine Books, 1994), and Daniel J. Kindlon and Michael Thompson, *Raising Cain: Protecting the Emotional Lives of Boys* (New York: Ballantine, 1998), for manifestations of North American's gendered culture on the lives of boys and girls.

11. Mercer, *GirlTalk*.

ministry.[12] We ask students who are in seminary to become youth ministers, Christian educators, or pastors to interview two youth and report on their findings. We provide a list of sample questions and basic guidelines for conducting open-ended, semi-structured, one-on-one interviews. We include questions that will prompt youth to talk about topics such as their own emerging identity, their relationship to church, their family of origin, and their sense of vocation. The interviewers are instructed to create a hospitable environment in which the young person is invited to feel as though "all the time in the world" is at their disposal.

Invariably, the class session in which these interviews are reported is a peak moment in the course. The reporting is accompanied by enthusiastic comments such as "She had never told anyone this story!" "He was so appreciative of our time together!" "I want to interview my whole youth group now!" Through repeated use of this assignment, we came to understand the "ethnographic listener" as one of several "functional models of the religious educator" that can be fruitfully incorporated into the youth minister's repertoire.[13]

Close analysis of Cara's interview, supported by the anecdotal reports of students who interview youth, shows that the private-yet-public moment-in-time of the interview deserves replication in the real world. Realizing the time constraints on any paid church worker, we do not imagine that youth ministers could interview every youth in their care. Rather, we encourage youth ministers to consider interviewing youth at particular moments, for instance, several months after a life experience that might launch an evolutionary leap in a youth's spiritual life. In the course of their high school and college years, youth and young adults experience crisis moments, which may become precursors to spiritual growth. The death of a friend, the

---

12. We are individually grateful to separate colleagues for introducing us to the benefit of this assignment. Dori thanks Dr. Evelyn Parker and Dr. Reginald Blount, colleagues in the Northwestern University Ph.D. program. Joyce thanks Dr. James W. Fowler.

13. Timothy Arthur Lines, *Functional Images of the Religious Educator* (Birmingham: Religious Education Press, 1992).

divorce of parents, a move to a new town, an injury affecting one's athletic endeavors, or the end of a significant friendship might prompt shifts in meaning-making. In addition to crisis events, mountaintop experiences such as a retreat, mission trip, or state basketball championship provide impetus for thinking about God in light of one's life experience.

Out of such events, both positive and negative, emerges testimony as we talk to one another in the course of our everyday lives and ministries. We suggest that on certain occasions the structure and formality of inviting an "interview" might provide a way of deepening the listening, opening wider the listener's voice, and claiming the moment of spiritual growth, doubt, questioning, or awakening. Out of such experiences of careful listening, wider understandings of holy listening might emerge.

We encourage youth ministers who have experienced the power of the youth interview to foster an ethos of holy listening among all who minister to youth, including volunteers and peers. By training youth and adult volunteers to hone their skills of holy listening and to name emerging life stories as potentially significant testimony, one might create an ethos in which it is perfectly acceptable and normal for small groups of listeners to focus on one youth and their story for a period of time. This kind of "listening circle," akin to Quaker practices, might be initiated by a youth following a time of growth or crisis, or might be suggested by a trusted leader or friend who has witnessed the life-changing event as a bystander or companion.

Sometimes holy listening uncovers despair, loss of hope, loss of faith, or depression. Embracing the questions and doubts that surface is vitally important, as is seeking appropriate interventions if therapeutic needs arise.

The urgency of evoking testimony in youth

Longstanding traditions of spiritual formation, along with the work of developmental theorists and ethnographic researchers, support this turn toward "ethnographic listening" as both a metaphor and a practical guide for youth ministry.

Quaker writer Douglas V. Steere describes the kind of listening that takes place within spiritual direction as similar to what I imagine Cara might have felt at the end of her interview:

> Have you ever sat with a friend when in the course of an easy and pleasant conversation the talk took a new turn and you both listened avidly to the other and to something that was emerging in your visit? You found yourselves saying things that astonished you and finally you stopped talking and there was an immense naturalness about the long silent pause that followed. In the silent interval you were possessed by what you had discovered together. If that has happened to you, you know that when you come up out of such an experience, there is a memory of rapture and a feeling in the heart of having touched holy ground.[14]

Steere distinguishes between this kind of holy listening and the kind of listening we tend to encounter most of the time. In the former, the focus remains on the speaker as the listener practices a disciplined posture of care, hospitality, relaxed awareness, and attentiveness. In most of our daily conversations, the listener is only listening with the "outer ear" and is inwardly preparing a response. In the holy listening Steere describes, the listener hones the capacity to "hear through many wrappings" and thereby fosters a climate in which "the most unexpected disclosures occur that are in the way of being miracles in one sense, and the most natural and obvious things in the world in another."

The value of evoking such testimony cannot be underestimated. Thomas Long writes:

> If a person has had a powerful religious experience, some deep meeting with holy mystery, whether this involves the birth of a child, a sudden moment of clarity, or a vision in the night, there

---

14. Douglas V. Steere, *Gleanings: A Random Harvest* (Nashville: Upper Room, 1986), 73.

are some things that can be said about it, but there are some parts of it that are ineffable, at least for the time being. If this person can say nothing at all about the experience, it will soon be lost, even to the one who had it.[15]

Sharon Daloz Parks, writing about the quest for adult faith, notes the importance of "communities of confirmation and contradiction" with whom to test new truths. She notes:

Transformation of our knowing and trusting is not complete until the new insight comes to voice and finds a place of confirmation within a wider public life. . . . The interpretive moment of testimony is essential, not simply as the completion of an inner process but also as participation in the forum of common experience that alone can confirm or refute the capacity of the image to grasp the real.[16]

Ethnographic researchers have often exclaimed with wonder that the interview space is "holy ground" in which both listener and speaker are changed. Margaret Ann Crain and Jack L. Seymour voiced the shift that happens when ethnographic research becomes ministry. They found this occurring when the ethnographer honors people's stories, creates a hospitable place for those stories to be heard alongside faith traditions, ands helps people clarify the meanings that organize their living. This process opens the speaker to critical thinking around their stories, and finally to deeper engagement in communities of wholeness and justice.[17] They write:

Almost every interview ended with the words thank you. We thanked these persons for inviting us onto the holy grounds of their lives. They thanked us because they found a time and a

---

15. Thomas G. Long, *Testimony: Talking Ourselves into Being Christian* (San Francisco, Jossey-Bass, 2004), 148.

16. Parks, *Big Questions, Worthy Dreams*, 121.

17. Margaret Ann Crain and Jack L. Seymour, "The Ethnographer as Minister," *Religious Education* 91 (Summer 1998): 312.

place to question, to reflect, and to express how they are seeking to connect faith with life.[18]

Joyce named a variety of constructive ways in which the YTI girls she researched made use of the interview, benefiting from the one-on-one attention, which may be especially important within a feminist perspective.

Without a space to speak her story, these experiences might remain implicit as well as the connections and new perspectives emerging out of them. . . . For girls with closely held beliefs, the one-on-one encounter with a listener provided a safe space to try out new perspectives emerging in the encounter with difference, away from the need to defend a point of view before peers or to save face. . . . The interview structured the opportunity for her to speak what she knew, and in so doing, to clarify it for herself.[19]

Finally, the urgency of such listening is highlighted by Steere, who writes: "To 'listen' another's soul into a condition of disclosure and discovery may be almost the greatest service that any human being ever performs for another." He reminds us that "over the shoulder" of the human listener there is the presence of the "eternal listener."[20]

This is an especially apt reminder in counseling youth toward vocational calling. It is not the listener who provides the answer, for there are no external authorities on life's deep issues. However, a host of attentive listeners might help youth come to trust their own inner voice and discover their own inner wisdom.

---

18. Margaret Ann Crain and Jack L. Seymour, *Yearning for God: Reflections of Faithful Lives* (Nashville, Upper Room, 2003), 154.

19. Mercer, *GirlTalk*.

20. Steere, *Gleanings*. I am grateful to Marjorie Thompson for pointing out this essay during a lecture entitled "The Listening Soul" given on October 23, 2004, at the Clergy Retreat for the Virginia Annual Conference of The United Methodist Church.

Hearing youth into vocation

Youth who ponder their purpose in life echo the poet's question: "Whom can I ask what I came to make happen in this world?" People of faith engaged in ministry with young people might discern two implicit assumptions in this quest: (1) that one's life is intended to have purpose beyond self-fulfillment and material gain; (2) that someone stands at the ready to help one discover that purpose.

These assumptions are in keeping with the ethical mandate of communities seeking to incarnate the body of Christ. However, our experiences as teens, young adults, seminary students, pastors, researchers, and seminary professors reflect that church communities often fail to live up to these assumptions. Churches do not always help youth articulate the religious dimensions of their call, often settling by default to support a more comfortable, less challenging quest for self-fulfillment and material well-being.

Sometimes, however, the church does rise to its high calling. It engages young people in the life-shaping practices of the Christian faith. Community forms and trust develops. These faith communities provide challenging exposure to the world, buffered by safe spaces that encourage the unfolding of a young person's unique gifts, talents, abilities, and desires. In communities such as this, young persons might find the "whom" to hear them into clarity about what they are supposed to be doing, both now and in the future.

The epigraph to this chapter reads: "Only in one's mother tongue can one express one's own truth. In a foreign language the poet dies." When the listener and the speaker share a common language, steeped in the particular experiences of a community in the act of forming itself around commitments to God's purposes in the world, one can express one's own radically fresh truth. Such was the case with Cara and the adult who interviewed her. It is also often the case within faith communities. Those journeying authentically through the practices of the Christian faith come to share a common language built on common experiences, common scripture, and a common milieu.

It is with each other that perhaps they will best be able to hear the poetic, the liminal, and the precocious testimony straining toward new realities of what Christians, as empowered individuals and communities, might offer the world. Holy listening as exemplified in Cara's interview (and potentially re-created in wider venues of youth ministry) invites the speaker into a space where she might wonder aloud about her life experience, faith journey, and sense of vocation. This type of listening engages the faith community in reclaiming the ancient Christian practice of testimony as a communal task with potential to reshape the public sphere.

•

In the next chapter, we will meet characters in six contemporary films. Their stories lend themselves to conversation around vocation as it relates to gender. We will meet boys like Napoleon Dynamite, who listens to his heart and fosters relationship in a hostile habitat. We will meet girls like Pai, born to lead her male-dominated tribe, and Jess, who prefers the forbidden world of soccer to preparing for marriage. Everywhere we look we will find girls being girls and boys being boys — but necessarily in ways we expect it. Napoleon, Jess, Pai and others may help youth see their own lives as stories worth living in refreshing new ways — ways that enlarge our visions of masculinity and femininity while contributing to *all* creation's flourishing.

Chapter 5

Stories worth living

To see that your life is a story while you're in the middle of living it may be a help to living it well.[1]

It's movie night at the Pura Vida Café. In a strip shopping center on the outskirts of Richmond, Virginia, four teens loosely affiliated with St. Luke's United Methodist Church gather around a table where Sam, a retired school principal, is sitting. Andrew, the youth minister at St. Luke's, is cueing up his portable DVD player. They order Costa Rican coffee, fill their water bottles, and curl their bodies into comfortable viewing position.

Andrew has brought *Napoleon Dynamite*, which Ben has seen six times. Sarah and her mom walk in from soccer practice, and the group makes room for them around the table. They chuckle at the opening credits, where a plate of tater tots and a peanut butter sandwich introduce the actors. They spend the next ninety minutes engrossed in the film, periodically interrupted by bathroom breaks, text messaging, outbursts of laughter, and stragglers joining their ranks.

As the film ends, conversation begins. Slowly at first, but picking up tempo as Sarah interrupts Katie and Ben interjects. Steered by Andrew, the group discusses the feelings which the film evoked in them and the characters with whom they identified. Katie remembers a lonely feeling during the first week of middle school, when she walked into the cafeteria each day and stared out at a sea of unfriendly faces. "I hated that feeling. It's the worst feeling in the world." The others join in, sharing their various connections with

---

1. Ursula Le Guin, *Gifts* (New York: Harcourt, 2004), 15.

characters in the film. "Where did you find God in this film?" Andrew asks, turning the conversation in a new direction. Ben refers to the lunchroom scene, when for the first time Napoleon, Deb, and Pedro sit together, instead of floundering alone. God is in that moment when community begins to form out of nothing, he says. Sarah recites the sentence Napoleon says to Pedro at the film's climax: "Just follow your heart, Pedro. That's what I do." God is in that moment, she says, because Napoleon listens to his inner voice, and urges Pedro to do the same. "I like the fact that Napoleon still looks like a freak at the end of the movie," Sam says. "Usually the nerdy kid gets transformed in this kind of plot. But here, God uses Napoleon just as he is."

The adults join in occasionally, but also hold back, finding delight in hearing the uninhibited banter of the teens. The conversation wraps up with Andrew asking "So what? What about this film will change the way you act in the world?" Ben scrunches up his face and heaves a heavy sigh. "Napoleon's so confident. He's too stupid to be afraid of appearing stupid. I guess it makes him a better person, not afraid of reaching out." Sarah chimes in. "It gives me one small glimpse of the way it *could* be. I mean, high school doesn't have to be one long, ugly contest to determine who's the coolest, does it?" As they clear the table and prepare to go home, Andrew tells them that next week they'll be watching *Whale Rider.*

Andrew has engaged his youth group in an intergenerational study of vocation, using carefully selected films to raise complicated questions around what it means for young women and men to offer their lives, to live authentically, and to find their purpose in the world.[2]

---

2. I (Dori) am grateful to Jason Stanley a Christian educator who regularly engages teens in the practice of critically engaging film using this method, for sharing this story with me. Names have been changed because the vignette offered here is representative, not the result of an actual session. It is important for adults facilitating this method to stay as much as possible in the question-asking mode, allowing the film to speak for itself, rather than providing pre-determined interpretations for youth.

A gendered approach to vocation

Vocation, as we have treated it so far in this volume, refers to an already/not-yet unfolding of one's particular contributions to the world. When carefully discerned and nurtured in community, a person's gifts and talents might bear fruit as a life offered to God to create a world of peace and justice, in keeping with the life and message of Jesus Christ. Youth have vocations in the here-and-now, not just in the future. Vocation is not just an individual quest, but a task best carried out in the company of friends. We envision this as a companioned walk between youth and adults.

Often missing from conversations around vocation is the issue of *gender*. Recent decades have birthed a heightened awareness of cultural stereotypes regarding beauty, thinness, and subservience that do not well serve the flourishing of adolescent girls. Less noted but equally damaging to the human community are stereotypes that narrow male aspiration to wealthy sports celebrities, violent street fighters, or dumb-and-dumber specimens willing to engage in testosterone-extreme contests. Many contemporary films continue to present such banal narratives of gendered identity. Teens who consume these films as part of their entertainment diet are ingesting a curriculum of vocation — a mainstream storyline telling them what they should look like, act like, think like, buy like, and aspire to be like as they grow into adult roles, male and female.

While contemporary culture emerging from Hollywood is easy for Christians to bemoan, it can also provide rich resources for faith formation. Some of the most creative, challenging, evocative, and potentially transformative narratives a youth might encounter reside within films. These cultural products, when reflected upon critically and in community, help youth imagine their own lives as stories being lived. Fictive characters create pathways to the real experiences of young women and men in the process of constructing identity in the here and now.

What follows is one way for adults to enter into theological reflection with youth around the Christian tradition of vocation. It is a way that is steeped in stories gleaned from popular culture in the form of movies with thick, complicated plotlines. It is a way, therefore, that is like life itself, far from neat and tidy.

We have chosen six films that offer glimpses of young men and women whose vocations emerge. These films do not present neatly packaged object lessons on Christian values. Rather, in each of these films, the characters make contributions to their communities in ways that open us to question gender's role in shaping our actions in the world. We can allow these characters — in their sometimes messy processes of unfolding vocation — to speak to us in our own joys and struggles of discerning God's call. The films are *Rabbit Proof Fence, Bend it Like Beckham, Whale Rider, Holes, 50 First Dates*, and *Napoleon Dynamite*.

The DVD player is cued. The film clips are ready to roll. But first, we must set the scene, developing the theme of gender as it relates to vocation. We will then introduce these films and their enticing characters. We conclude by exploring a method of theological reflection that encourages critical thinking about the films and the meanings they evoke, especially in light of the venerable concept of vocation rooted in the Hebrew community and given full voice by the Protestant reformers.

Re-dressing gender: A world out of balance

Conversation around gender equality uses categories that are problematic. To compare the plight of girls and boys, women and men, entails a separation that belies much of what we know about how identity is formed. However, the constructs of gender still operate to shape us. The categories, while limited, nonetheless enable us to push at their edges, creating navigable spaces in which to consider the way gender shapes vocational ambitions.

Girls are surpassing boys on standardized college admission tests and in admittance to prestigious colleges. Girls are being raised with the implicit assumption that they can become whatever they want when they grow up. Many have entered fields formerly accessible only to men. Despite the fact that men make more money than women in the workplace and still outrank women in positions of authority, the past quarter-century has birthed huge advances in the potential of girls and women.[3] While other features that intersect with gender such as race and class continue to set limits on girls and their potential, many markers reflect positive gains.

But the aims of feminism cannot be reduced to quantifiable comparisons between men and women, boys and girls, without missing the mark. Concerns for women's equality were indeed about creating girls who are smart, strong, and bold, *but not at the expense of boys.* Current data compiled by the Search Institute tell us that boys are more likely to be incarcerated, to commit homicide, and to be victims of violent crime. Boys are more likely than girls to have chronic conditions such as asthma, to be diagnosed with learning disabilities, and to drop out of school. Boys are less likely than girls to volunteer and to express being spiritually grounded.[4] In short "while we have expanded acceptable options for girls and women in such spheres as sports and business, we haven't done as well at inviting boys and men to explore personal interests that emphasize relationships, caring, and creative expression. Cultural norms tell boys that such interests aren't masculine."[5]

In addition to a narrowing of life options for both boys and girls that sometimes gets determined by gender, there is the issue of balancing work, reproduction, and family nurture. In observing the lives of young women, we often see that their young adulthoods — including college and advanced degrees — prepare them for a highly skilled plunge into career, often just at the moment they decide to hit the "Pause" button to pursue having and raising children. One of us was recently dismayed to hear a physician who trains medical school residents bemoan the fact that a doctor he had trained had carved

---

3. Eugene C. Roehlkepartain, "Connecting with Boys: Closing the Asset Gap," The Magazine of Ideas for Healthy Communities and Healthy Youth, Summer, 2001, (*www.search-institute.org*), 1.

4. Ibid.

5. Ibid.

out a part-time work life so as to be present to her young children. "What a waste of a highly skilled resource," he said, giving voice to the assumption that rearing children holds little value compared to a medical career. Choosing to take time out of career — for men or women — to be present to the task of child-rearing is often undervalued in our society. These choices, therefore, are hard to justify and often bring with them the burden of angst over peak years "wasted" in the daily difficulties and joys of raising young children.

Our current world — at risk of ecological destruction, awash in war, and plagued by vast inequalities between the haves and have-nots — reflects an imbalance between genders. We've divvied up what it means to be human, and both males and females have suffered the consequences.

Christian tradition envisions a different way, a way of being in the world that sees mutuality, distinctiveness, and community as central to the good life. It is that vision — sometimes spoken of as the peace-able kin-dom — to which we now turn. We have chosen these six films because, in ways large and small, they show young men and women acting out their vocations in the world in ways that enlarge our notions of what it means to be masculine or feminine, thereby contributing to the flourishing of *all* creation.

Turning to stories:
The curriculum of vocation as evoked in six films

Recently, I (Dori) finished reading *Old Yeller* with my daughter. As we approached the ending, both suspecting the death of the beloved dog but not knowing for sure, she said to me "Mom, let's read this chapter out loud so we can have our feelings *together*." Before moving on, we talked about possible endings and what the author may have wanted to accomplish. "Is it better for him to protect kids from sadness by letting the dog live? Or is there value in walking us through a really sad event so it might help us later?" I asked. Laughing, she said "Protect us! Protect us! Let us be kids a while longer!" In reflecting later about this exchange, I realized that reading this work of fiction together was a fitting way for my daughter and me to "practice" grief in anticipation of life's inevitable non-fictive griefs.

It is this lived belief in the power of stories to teach that brings us to the films at hand. Unlike books, through which we usually embark on solitary emotional journeys, films can allow us to "have the feelings together." Fostering emotional literacy is a critical intervention that youth ministry can make, especially into the lives of boys for whom the development of an emotional repertoire may have been subtly discouraged.[6]

When viewed and discussed at a congregational gathering involving youth, these films will tease out interrelated themes of vocation and gender. These themes emerge slowly and in part, in dialogue and increasing complexity, in multiple layers of meaning accessible to both a highly articulate seventeen-year-old senior, as well as a younger, less-mature middle-schooler. Keeping in mind both of these imaginary youth, we walk into the storied universe of contemporary film.

We suggest using these films as part of an ongoing series, either over the course of a retreat, over the course of a six-week movie club, or interspersed intentionally throughout the year, preferably as part of an intergenerational gathering including youth.[7] Following brief descriptions of the films, we describe a method of theological reflection that can be used to engage them as teaching tools.

---

6. For a helpful discussion of the ways parents engage in emotional steering that subtly discourage boys from exploring feelings, see Daniel J. Kindlon and Michael Thompson, *Raising Cain: Protecting the Emotional Life of Boys* (New York: Ballantine, 1999), 17ff.

7. All six of these films are rated PG or PG-13. We recommend pre-screening films before viewing them with youth. Both *Bend It Like Beckham* and *50 First Dates* contain brief scenes that might be deemed offensive. These can be screened out using a parental control feature without affecting appreciation of the plot. Of the two, *50 First Dates* includes more questionable material. We include it despite reservations about these scenes because of its value as a counter-narrative to predominant romance plots. In our estimation, its overall theme contains sufficient value to override its moments of crude humor.

Three of these films provide glimpses of young women pursuing portions of their life's calling, despite strong resistance from family, culture, and society. In each of these films, girls are living out vocations that traditionally would be deemed masculine. The other three films depict young men who exhibit deeply relational gifts as creators of community, caretakers of the weak, and patient navigators of life's devastating losses — characteristics typically deemed feminine. We treat them in pairs that reflect intentional grouping of cohering themes.

Walk it: Rabbit Proof Fence *and* Holes

In the movie *Rabbit Proof Fence,* three young Aboriginal girls are abducted from their families, who live in the outback of Western Australia. They are taken by force to a boarding school as part of a plan to assimilate half-castes into the majority population. A human rights committee of the United Nations investigated this policy and reported that from 10 to 30 percent of all Australian Aborigines were forcibly removed from their families under these policies between the years of 1930 and 1970. The film is based on the committee's report, entitled *Bringing Them Home.*[8]

The three girls, led by the eldest Molly, escape from the camp and manage to evade their pursuers, who use advanced technology in their efforts to recapture the escapees. By following the rabbit-proof fence — erected to keep a rabbit plague from spreading — two of the girls manage to return to their families. Their skills as trackers and their innate connection to the natural environment assist them on their homeward journey.

---

8. Although the movie is based in fact, much controversy surrounds the film and the report on which it was based. In introducing the film, it is important to inform viewers that this depiction is told from one perspective, around which there is disagreement. A differing interpretation of the historical events is that the Aboriginal people expressed a desire to assimilate to mainstream culture. Key to this interpretation is the view that access to consumer goods would be available only if younger generations gained entrée into the economy's workforce.

This film gifts us with a girl in the role of courageous liberator. Molly is a public resister launching a movement toward freedom. She is a Moses figure, following her calling to lead her comrades along a danger-filled path with no certain outcome. She perseveres through extreme conditions, following her instincts and using her finely honed skills to avoid detection.

The movie *Holes* also involves a long trek toward freedom. Stanley Yelnats IV, the main character, is a hard-luck kid wrongly accused of stealing a pair of sneakers. Sent to a juvenile detention center in the Texas desert, Yelnats learns that he doesn't have to live by the harsh every-man-for-himself conditions of the camp. He befriends a younger boy, nicknamed Zero, teaching him to read. Subtly, he subverts the cruelly competitive ethos in favor of a cooperative one. As the narrative progresses, Yelnats's move toward friendship launches him into the roles of both mentor and liberator.

With little hope of surviving, the two boys escape during the heat of the day, setting their sights on "God's Thumb," a rocky promontory in the far distance that promises water. During their long journey, two subplots unfold through flashbacks. One involves a tragic story of a love between a white woman and a black man that ended in his lynching. The result was a long harsh drought that turned a lush lakeside community into the desert over which the two boys are walking. Interwoven into this story is the tale of Stanley's no-account-pig-stealing-great-great-grandfather, whose thanklessness is redeemed by Stanley's compassionate solidarity with Zero.

This film models masculinity in the form of caring for the weak. Stanley subverts a violent regime through a small act of kindness. This kindness grows in him, creating a kind of leadership that honors relationship and refuses to see persons as expendable. In the world of survival created by Stanley, no one counts for "zero." In this light, Zero begins to see himself as someone with a story to tell and a life to offer.

Taken together, these films show young persons in the act of walking a path for which they are uniquely suited. If they chose not to pursue their callings, freedom from oppressive systems would not occur. Stanley and Molly persuasively act in ways that serve to re-balance skewed visions of masculine and feminine. The example of boys who are emotionally tender and girls who are cleverly shrewd might encourage viewers to include these capacities in their own life-repertoires.

The fact that the two films are jarringly different in genre and style make them good companions. *Rabbit Proof Fence* is haunting and disturbing. In contrast, *Holes* manages to be uplifting, despite an oppressive climate and disturbing subject matter. Both movies raise the issue of white racism, providing vastly different perspectives from which to enter conversation about it.

Ride it: Whale Rider *and* Napoleon Dynamite

In the movie *Whale Rider,* a young girl named Paikea (Pai for short) follows an inner voice that is contrary to her grandfather's wishes. Set in a small Maori village on the eastern shore of New Zealand, the film begins with a birth narrative reminiscent of the biblical stories of Moses and Jesus. Pai's mother and twin brother, who as the firstborn grandson of the tribal chief had been anticipated as a future leader, die in childbirth. Pai alone survives. Her grieving father flees home, but not before naming his daughter after Paikea, the tribal ancestor who supposedly arrived at the village on the back of a whale.

The grandfather, Koro, practically abandons Pai in the delivery room, muttering "What use is a girl?" Pai grows to be a sensitive and solitary child, communing with nature, especially the whales, whose song she hears at night.

Over the years, Pai and her grandfather grow close. However, when Koro begins training the boys of the village in the ancient ways — looking among them for one who might lead — he forbids Pai's participation because she is a girl. A born leader, she spies on the boys' training sessions and seeks her uncle's warrior skills to gain the knowledge she desperately needs.

Pai's gifts are affirmed by her loving grandmother and slowly emerge to be recognized by a growing circle of others. When several whales beach themselves and are in danger of dying, the tribe rallies to save them. When all other efforts fail, Pai climbs atop a whale as the tide rises. She gently coaxes the whale back to the ocean, and the other whales follow. The final affirmation of Pai's calling eventually comes from the male chief. However, her community had begun to affirm her gift long before its official leader could see clearly her unique call.

Napoleon Dynamite is a different kind of loner. Physically unattractive and socially immature, he stumbles through his painful daily existence. His absentee grandmother leaves him in the care of a narcissistic uncle and older cousin. His daily journey through the halls of high school is filled with pain and angst. When newcomer Pedro, a Hispanic boy with a "sweet" bike, enrolls in school, Napoleon befriends him. Joined by the shy but friendly Deb, a small triangle of friendship begins.

Pedro decides to run for class president, challenging the popular blonde cheerleader Summer. As the election nears, Summer gives her candidate speech, followed by a skit in which the Happy Hands club dances. Pedro, unaware that a skit was expected, panics behind the stage. Napoleon gives him this advice: "Follow your heart, Pedro. That's what I do."

Pedro walks slowly to the podium, promises to erect holy saints in the hallways of the school and says "Vote for me and all your wildest dreams will come true." Behind the curtain, as Pedro speaks, Napoleon has improvised a plan to provide a skit. Dressed in his "Vote for Pedro" T-shirt, Napoleon shows off the dance moves he has been practicing behind his bedroom door. The dance impresses the student body crowded into the auditorium, eliciting a standing ovation. This small triangle of misfits finds a way to support one another, against seemingly insurmountable odds, and successfully challenges the shallow-lookism pervading their high school.

Whale Rider, a serious tale of spiritual longings, and *Napoleon Dynamite,* a goofy comedy about teenage misfits, have little in common. Pai rides the back of a whale: Napoleon rides a bicycle. They both ride into a void of leadership, filling it with their own particular gifts. Both Pai and Napoleon follow their hearts, allowing their callings to emerge, despite a hostile environment. While Pai's leadership is steeped in ancient ways and evokes a holy calling, Napoleon's leadership is indigenous to small-town Minnesota. What holiness we ascribe to Napoleon's ways of being in the world comes only as we infuse spirituality into ordinary life.

Pai gifts us with a version of leadership that emerges tentatively, in close connection to nature and in careful negotiation around valued relationships. Napoleon gifts us with a vision of a person in touch with his feelings, knowledgeable about matters of the heart, and able to create community out of almost nothing. In ways that seem natural, unforced, and totally believable, these two characters counteract the lingering "shoulds" regarding gender. Careful viewers might imagine the possibilities of life differently for having walked alongside Pai and Napoleon.

Bend It: Bend It Like Beckham *and* 50 First Dates

The main character of the movie *Bend It Like Beckham* is Jess, an English teenager of Indian descent. She is born to play soccer, but is forbidden to do so by her traditional parents, who want her to be more like her sister, Pinky. Pinky is busy planning a wedding to her Indian boyfriend and learning to cook Indian delicacies. As the wedding plans progress, Jess begins a secret life, stealing away to play on an all-girls soccer team. There her pick-up skills flourish under the tutelage of her coach, Joe, for whom she develops a crush. The idol plastered in posters on Jess's bedroom wall is Beckham, the English soccer star famous for kicking killer curve balls. From friends on the team, Jess learns of women's professional soccer, and aspires to win a scholarship to a U.S. college.

The film is rife with girl power and infused with religion. Before leaving the house bent on deception, Jess consults the Hindu icon centered above the living room fireplace, as if to garner his support.

Surreptitiously, Jess uses money intended for wedding shoes to buy a new pair of soccer shoes.

Jess's soccer playing is discovered. In addition, she is accused of being a lesbian, after being seen hugging her friend at a bus stop. When news of this spreads through the tight-knit Indian community, it threatens to destroy Pinky's wedding plans. The misunderstanding is cleared up, and Jess finally warms her father's heart. Conversation between them opens his old wounds over being excluded from soccer games during his youth because of his immigrant status. Finally, he consents to come to one of Jess's games.

In the climax of the movie, Jess's team is playing a tournament on the same day as Pinky's wedding. With her father's permission, Jess changes from her ornate sari into her soccer gear, dashing from the wedding hall to take her place on the field. The film then cuts back and forth between dancers at the wedding gala and girls on the soccer field, revealing the stark contrast between the sisters and their chosen paths in life.

Jess, sneaky and deceptive, is nevertheless a role model. She refuses to let traditional views about women limit her aspirations. While lying to one's parents is hardly commendable, Jess contributes to a rewriting of gender codes by resisting standards she finds to be oppressive.

The film *50 First Dates* stars Adam Sandler, best known for humor of the crudest sort. While this film does include difficult-to-watch moments that attempt to wring humor out of sexual subject matter, its poignant depiction of relationship in the midst of disability redeems it and makes it worth pondering.

Sandler's character, Henry Roth, is a Maui veterinarian with expertise in marine animals. Off the job, he is a womanizer specializing in short-term romances with female tourists — until he meets Lucy over breakfast one morning. They spend hours talking, and he finds himself smitten. They make plans to meet the next day, at which time Lucy doesn't remember Henry at all. He learns from the diner's owner that Lucy was in an accident that caused brain damage, leaving her with short-term amnesia. Each night when she sleeps, her slate is wiped clean and she remembers nothing of the day before. Her father and brother concoct a fantasy to make each day feel the same, so as not to force her to deal with the pain of the accident again and again.

Contrary to the wishes of Lucy's father, Henry begins elaborate schemes to get Lucy to remember him and to return the growing affection he feels for her. As he spends time with Lucy, he becomes transformed. He no longer sees women as expendable. Rather, he finds himself willing to delay his own dreams to pursue a relationship that entails helping her deal with this disability.

He begins making a video to inform Lucy of the events of the day before and their growing friendship. She watches the video first thing each morning to bring herself up-to-date. After realizing that he has put his life on hold for her, Lucy begins to feel guilty. "Don't you want to have a career?" she asks him. "A family? A life?" Determined that caring for her is incompatible with his having a life, she ends the relationship and goes to live at an institute for people with conditions similar to her own. There she occupies herself by teaching art to her fellow patients.

Henry, dealing with grief over the break-up, renovates his old sailboat and prepares to take a long-planned trip to Antarctica to study penguins. Before departing, he decides to visit Lucy at the institute. He finds her in the art room, surrounded by paintings of the man who appears each night in her dreams. Although she doesn't recognize Henry when she sees him, all of the paintings reflect his countenance.

At the film's end, Lucy has not miraculously recovered. She still must watch the *Good Morning, Lucy* video at the start of each day to orient herself. But because of Henry's persistence and creativity in the face of her disability, Lucy is able to have a life that is rich and meaningful.

Henry and Jess are likable characters. They bend gender roles in small ways, welcome ways, ways that are both personal and political. I suspect teen viewers might easily embrace Henry and Jess as healers, both of relationships and of the world.

•

These six films help us envision young women and men creating lives that contribute to the well-being of the world.

The vast canon of Western literature is full of stories of young men embarking on quests that change the world. Harder to find are stories of males who foster community, create harmony, or counter violence. These stories, when we find them, deserve to be celebrated as moments that break down gendered norms of masculinity, welcoming the creative expression of longings that extend beyond the boundaries expected by traditional scripts.

Similarly, it is easy to recall films depicting brave women who create a nurturing home life while men are away at war or accumulating wealth. Stories of females who eschew fashion and tradition to follow their callings out in the world, while increasingly available, are still somewhat rare. Even when they do exist, they still get co-opted by the male gaze. This collection of films depicts young women in highly particular contexts contesting norms determined by race, gender, and traditional religious scripts.

Women and men raised with flexible understandings of gender have obviously come of age. They are now making films that hold the power to nurture the flourishing of today's youth, girls and boys. Harvesting these films for theological meaning is a process akin to reminding African Americans of their rich cultural heritage in the form of spirituals and slave narratives. That process, so richly illuminated by Anne Streaty Wimberly, informs this use of films as cultural artifacts worthy of theological reflection with youth.[9]

It is important to remember that Hollywood likes happy endings. All of these films resolve on a high note, instilling hope and creating that warm, fuzzy feeling that will bring us back to the Cineplex. Life is typically more ambivalent. Our own glimpses of meaning are partial, filled with devastating setbacks out of our control, and often put on

---

9. Anne Streaty Wimberly, *Soul Stories: African American Christian Education* (Nashville: Abingdon, 1994). See also Yolanda Smith, *Reclaiming the Spirituals: New Possibilities for African American Christian Education* (Cleveland: Pilgrim Press, 2004).

hold because of poverty, unjust systems of oppression, or debilitating illnesses such as depression.

Christians, unlike fictive characters in a movie, make choices about how we spend our time. We can choose to cultivate communities of compassion. We can foster the capacity to sit with one another through life's painful places. As we emerge from our movie nights into the stark light of our lived realities, we need to follow the way of Christ, who did not flee from illness, death, and untidy lives, but rather entered those places willingly and urges us to join him there. It is in Christ's ministries of love and justice that we find the urges, longings, and directives that can guide our callings.

Story theology:
A method of theological reflection on films

In a narrative pedagogy using theological reflection, these films would be watched in a group setting, preferably including both youth and adults. After each film, participants would engage in a process of theological reflection involving a four-step method I (Dori) have detailed elsewhere as Girlfriend Theology, but adapt here to be gender inclusive, to focus on a fictional narrative, and to consciously interject particular content of the Christian tradition. The process follows this pattern:[10]

1. Watch the film or selected clips.

2. Discuss the questions: What feelings did you have during the film? With which characters did you most strongly identify? What portions of your own life did you see reflected here? Did it remind you of any specific stories from your own experience?

3. Discuss the questions: Where is God in this story? What images of God from scripture, tradition, or your own experience emerge?

---

10. Dori Grinenko Baker, *Doing Girlfriend Theology: God-Talk with Young Women* (Cleveland: Pilgrim Press, 2005).

How do these images of God fit with or challenge your current understandings about God? What Christian practice does this story illuminate? How do the characters in this story help us proceed along the way of Christ?

4. Prepare to go forth by asking the question "What difference does this story and our reflection on it make?" Did you have any "aha" moments during the discussion? What specific ways might you live differently for having watched this movie and taken part in this discussion?

A key undercurrent throughout this discussion is the conviction that the quest for authentic vocation and identity occurs not only in adolescence, but nags many practicing Christians throughout our lives. For this reason, this process of theological reflection is greatly enriched by the presence of adults who carefully interject teachable moments in which they make explicit the alternative curriculum of vocation we are suggesting throughout this book, and who also are willing to learn from and with youth about vocation.

This process, when engaged around specific narratives that open to themes of vocation and gender, supports this alternative curriculum of vocation by:

- expanding the self-awareness of youth from that of uncritical consumers of culture to that of producers of meaning and agents of transformation in the current world, not simply in the future;

- allowing youth to practice the vocabulary of call and vocation inherited from scripture and Protestant reformers;

- encouraging youth to understand vocation as both a private quest and an inherently public task — one in which the baptized community provides connection to the transcendent reality that calls one's gifts forward and fosters good stewardship of them;

- illustrating gender as a realm of freedom in which activities such as caretaking of relationships, public leadership, nurturing of community, and subversion of violence are essentially human tasks, shared between males and females.

Contemporary films have a short shelf life. While some become cult classics, others lose their freshness and their ability to speak to youth within a year of their release. For this reason, these six films serve merely as examples of how a narrative pedagogy involving theological reflection based on film might work. We encourage adults who work with youth to constantly scan the horizon of popular culture, adding to their teaching repertoire new releases that similarly help evoke the curriculum of vocation at the center of Christian faith.

Gender literacy

In this chapter, we have seen that gender shapes us, even as we re-shape notions of gender by our particular ways of being male and female. Films provide tangible narratives upon which we can focus the lens of gender. When we do so repeatedly with young people, we may see emerging "gender literacy." This connotes the ability to reflect critically about gendered norms and stereotypes, especially those that limit vocational imagination in both youth and adults. Gender literacy implies the possibility of creating new pathways of being masculine and feminine.

Our move toward gender literacy continues in the next two chapters, which look at the stories that lie close to the center of who we are as deeply relational creatures of a relational God. In chapter 6, we'll see the ways parents can support the vocational strivings of their teenaged daughters. Then we will turn to guys' stories, looking for ways that the church might help them lead more fulfilling lives.

Chapter 6

Like Job's daughters
Parents, vocation, and adolescent girls

Julie talks with many adults in her life about her desire to make a difference in the world. As an honor student living in a small, somewhat isolated mill town in the mountains of the southeastern United States, Julie has grown up hearing from teachers and counselors at school that she can "go anywhere and do anything" and that she "ought to get out of here, attend a good college somewhere, and make something of" herself and her life.

When Julie reflects on the messages she has received in school and church, she notes that many adults around her focus on her academic abilities as the ticket to escape the kind of life they lead in their small town. "I know they mean it for good, because they don't want me to be stuck with the same kinds of limits that they have in their lives and work. And I'm sure it's more exciting out there somewhere, like in New York City or Washington."

Julie's parents offer similar encouragements to go out into the wider world. But, says Julie, her parents also talk to her about "keeping faith with where you've come from," and how "what you do matters, but who you are when you do it matters even more." What they mean, Julie explains, is that "if I go out there to some fancy college or law school and get a big important job, but am not a kind person, an honest person, a good person, the difference I can make in the world will be just as limited as folks here who feel trapped in their factory jobs."

Expressing her observation that the opportunities available to women and girls in her town are narrower than those for men and boys, Julie compares herself to the daughters of Job (chapter 42) who are unusual among women in the Hebrew Bible because unlike so many biblical women they are named in the text (Jemimah, Keziah, and Kerenhappuch, Job 42:14). They also receive an inheritance from their father Job. "I am like Job's daughters, the ones who got to have a share of their father's wealth even though they were girls. My parents are like that with me. They don't want me to end up like so many other girls here, having babies young and working in the factory for practically nothing. They say especially for girls it matters to reach high. My mom wants a better life for me than the one she feels she has had, because she thinks her work is boring and she doesn't get paid much, especially as a woman. She is worried about how girls get stuck in this town, how they can only be certain things or work in certain kinds of jobs here because they are girls.

"But the thing she communicates the most to me is that I can make a difference for good wherever I am and whatever I'm doing. I might go someplace else for a while. But I plan to come back here, to try to make a difference here somehow. My teachers are important, my counselor at school helps me think about college in ways my parents can't [because they did not go to college]. But I think the people with the biggest influence on what I do with my life are my parents. They want me to do some kind of good work, different than they could do, but they also show me all the time that there are lots of ways to matter in the world."

In this chapter, we focus specifically on girls, parents, and vocation. What kind of influence do mothers and fathers have on the vocational strivings of girls? Adolescent girls have been the subjects of considerable study and interest in the fields of psychology, education, and sociology. They have captured popular attention through books such as Mary Pipher's (1994) *Reviving Ophelia*. And yet in the literature of Christian youth ministry, adolescent girls remain understudied, poorly presented, and inadequately represented. At the same time, several studies look directly at the importance of gender in the faith experiences and moral lives of girls[1] Similarly, recent research by Christian Smith underscores the importance of parents in the lives of teens.[2]

In our interview research, we listened to teens talk about their relationships with their parents. Quite unexpectedly, we began to observe a pattern in these interviews, in which girls in particular spoke of the roles their parents played in forming their perspectives on vocation, especially (but not limited to) that aspect of vocation concerned with future work. As we listened to young women in conversations and interviews, we heard them describe widely varying levels of connection, closeness, disapproval, and appreciation of their parents. Several expressed significant tension and difficulty in their family relationships, many of which were complicated by dynamics of parental divorce

---

1. Notable exceptions to this include the following works, all of which are examples of academic writings focusing on young women: Evelyn Parker, *Trouble Don't Last Always: Emancipatory Hope among African Americans* (Cleveland: Pilgrim Press, 2003); Dori Grinenko Baker, *Doing Girlfriend Theology: God-Talk with Young Women* (Cleveland: Pilgrim Press, 2005); Patricia Davis, *Beyond Nice: The Spiritual Wisdom of Adolescent Girls* (Minneapolis: Fortress, 2001); Barbara Blodgett, *Constructing the Erotic: Sexual Ethics and Adolescent Girls* (Cleveland: Pilgrim Press, 2002); and various chapters with Jeanne Moessner's edited volume, *In Her Own Time: Women and Developmental Issues in Pastoral Care* (Minneapolis: Fortress Press, 2000). In popular youth ministry literature aimed principally at non-theologically educated practitioners, however, the subject of gender is missing in action, as are perspectives on the particularity of girls. See also Joyce Ann Mercer, "Gender, Violence and Faith: Adolescent Girls and a Theological Anthropology of Difference," Ph.D dissertation, Emory University, Atlanta, 1997; Carol Gilligan et al., *Mapping the Moral Domain: A Contribution of Women's Thinking to Psychological Theory and Education* (Cambridge, Mass.: Center for the Study of Gender Education and Human Development, 1988), Carol Gilligan, Nona Lyons, and Trudy Hanmor, eds., *Making Connections: The Relational World of Adolescent Girls at Emma Willard School* (Troy, N.Y.: Emma Willard School, 1989); Lyn Mikel Brown and Carol Gilligan, *Meeting at the Crossroads: Women's Psychology and Girls' Development* (Cambridge, Mass.: Harvard University Press, 1992), Patricia Davis, *Counseling Adolescent Girls* (Minneapolis: Fortress Press, 1996); Evelyn Parker, *The Sacred Selves of Adolescent Girls: Hard Stories of Race, Class, and Gender* (Cleveland: Pilgrim Press, 2006).
2. Christian Smith, with Melinda Lundquist Denton, *Soul-Searching: The Religious and Spiritual Lives of American Teenagers* (New York: Oxford University Press, 2005).

and/or remarriage. Other girls described relationships of deep affection, admiration, and emotional closeness with one or more parents.
Still others spoke of volatile, fluctuating levels of connection and
distance with parents.

Across all types of relationships, however, these girls all articulated
the significant influences and contributions made by their parents to
the shaping of their perspectives on their gifts and how they might
use their gifts both now and into the future. We hear in these conversations with girls three distinct patterns for how parents can "bless"
the vocational strivings of their adolescent daughters: Parents become
companions on the vocational journeys of their daughters by (1) believing in their daughters out loud; (2) living out their own gifts in
ways their daughters admire and value; and, (3) sometimes by a *via
negativa*, offering girls up-close examples of what they hope the girls
will *not* to do in their lives.

Believing in their daughters out loud

The first of these patterns of vocational blessing might best be called
simply "believing in their daughters out loud." Part of the story about
parenting told by these interviews is that many parents have faith
in their daughters' gifts, abilities, and commitments, but only some
make those beliefs known in ways that the girls can receive. Those
who do find ways to "believe in their daughters out loud" offer a
distinctive gift to the religious lives of these adolescent girls: in a time
of life and a social context that discourages girls from stepping into
the world with confidence and commitment, girls who have explicit
parental support for their vocational strivings get an extra boost of
confidence to buoy up their efforts. These interviews suggest that
fathers and mothers who openly affirmed their daughters' emerging
gifts, abilities, and explorations supported the vocational aspirations
of their daughters and imbued them with confidence to question,
explore, and try out new possibilities.

Lydia, for example, responding to a question of what kinds of
messages she received from her father about being a young woman,

said with enthusiasm, "He tells me all the time what a clever person I am and how great I am and how he loves me. My dad always tells me that I can do whatever I want to do, and that I will do it well. He says I have enough talent to do whatever I want, but that the main thing in life is to be able to do whatever God wants me to do. For Lydia, her father's belief in her abilities and desires, and his explicit connection of those with "whatever God wants me to do" offer an unequivocal blessing of her vocational strivings, even at a very tentative time before any particular career or educational path has become clear to her.

Significantly, Lydia reports these affirmations from her father not in response to a direct question about vocation, but in the context of an inquiry about gender messages. The unspoken subtext, then, involves messages from other sources which assert that because she is female, Lydia's vocational choices remain limited. In contrast to these, her father asserts that she is clever and talented and that "doing whatever God wants [her] to do" is the primary factor that should determine how she uses her life and gifts. By "believing in her out loud," Lydia's father blesses her with confidence that may help her to resist pressures from the wider society and even the church that she accept a narrow range of vocational options due to her gender.

At times, the act of parents "believing in their daughters out loud" came in the face of some particular experience of the girls feeling disempowered or held back by others. Katherine, who had sensed from an early age the call to the priesthood, at one point found herself being laughed at by her dance teacher at school because of her desires to become a priest: "She laughed at me when I said that I wanted to be a priest. . . . I was trying to confront her, and I was willing to talk it out with her . . . and she was like, 'Who do you dance for, huh? Who do you dance for?' And I said, 'I dance for God. I do everything for God.' And she started laughing. . . . And I told my mom about this, and my mom was just incensed. . . . She called the dean in." Katherine offered this incident in a description of her relationship with her mother, whom she described as "supporting whatever I want to do," and being willing to intervene with others who do not similarly support her vocational strivings. While she expressed a certain embarrassment about the confrontation that took place there, in which her mother forcefully asserted to the dean and the dance teacher that people like them in positions of authority do not have the right to make fun of their students' vocational choices, Katherine also clearly felt affirmed and supported by her mother in her vocational explorations and her understanding of her dance activities as being tied to her faith.

Sometimes, though, even the active advocacy of parents cannot offset the pull toward "de-selfing" — denying or downplaying gifts, abilities, and passions — that girls continue to experience. In the case of Melinda, who had moved from her birthplace in the Caribbean Islands to a new home and school in a Midwestern state in the United States, the demand to deny certain aspects of herself in order to be part of a racially defined peer group was expressed in her experiences in school, when she first met black students who were African American: "They thought that I was trying to act white because of the grades that I got. And that's when, those experiences, they just changed me completely. I realized that if I raised my hand that meant I knew the answer or that I was thinking, and they equated thinking with being white. And I didn't want to be called that. . . .

"I remember my first time interacting with black students that were, um, I don't know, they were really different. I remember this one young man, he came to me and he said he'd never go out with me . . . he was all, 'She doesn't look like us. . . . She doesn't know who she is. She's a sell-out. . . . ' And that's when I became an introvert . . . because I didn't want them to think that I was trying to act white by raising my hand, and so I kept all the answers to myself. And I'd just think about — what would happen was that I'd want to raise my hand to say the answer, but then I'd think. . . . 'Wait, should I say that? Will I be [perceived as being] too smart if I say something like that?' And so I didn't raise my hand. *Even though I kept on being reassured by my mother,* I didn't want others to think that [I was a sell-out]."

In a school setting where students constructed racial identity in terms of participation and non-participation in classroom activities,

Melinda chose to be identified with her black peers even at considerable cost. Her mother's encouragement of her intellectual abilities and reassurance about racial identity did not adequately subvert the pull for Melinda to take her intelligence underground for the sake of her desire to be accepted by an African American peer group.[3]

But Melinda made it clear elsewhere in her interview that her mother's support and affirmation played an important role in strengthening her ability to make good life choices. Asked how she goes about making important decisions in her life, Melinda replied, "I ask my mom first. No, I think about the pros and cons, and then I ask my mom. And—goodness—I always regret it, because she always gives me this psychoanalysis and she...never gives me a straightforward answer.... I'm like, 'What do you want me to do?' And she says, 'It's your decision.' After talking about all that! (laughs) And so then I ask God what is right, and then I decide. And most of my decisions have been pretty good." While she joked about regretting her mother's refusal to tell her what to do, Melinda evidenced a comfort level about her own decision-making abilities that were very much linked to her mother's expressed confidence in her. When parents communicate their belief in their daughters' gifts and abilities, they support those aspects of their daughters' religious lives tied to vocational seeking and decision-making.

Several of the girls spoke of experiencing parental disapproval or lack of understanding of their specific vocational interests in spite of their parents' overall affirmation of their abilities and gifts. Valerie,

---

3. We are not disputing or undermining the significance of race as a feature of identity. Rather, while racial identity obviously constituted an important aspect of selfhood for Melinda, the tragedy was that in her move to the United States, she encountered race constructed in such a way that she felt the necessity give up other vital aspects of her identity in order to claim her blackness, in effect trading off the costs of denying racial solidarity with those of denying her pleasure in learning and her intellectual gifts. We consider it an insidious feature of a racist society that youth of color make the internalization of the inferior identities granted them by majority culture groups into a form of resistance, a move that further perpetuates status distinctions. In the cases of many other girls of color with whom we have spoken or observed in classroom contexts, even the affirmation of parents and other adults often does not empower girls to make other choices.

for example, came to her summer experience at the Youth Theological Initiative (YTI) with extensive leadership experience in her church. She had already been serving as an elder at her Presbyterian church, a position of considerable responsibility. She voiced her interest in pursuing theological education after college in order to follow what she was exploring as a possible call to the ministry. But Valerie reported her efforts to share these vocational yearnings with her father as being the times she felt most distant from her father in what she described as an otherwise close relationship: "There are times, especially when talking about college, what I want to do with the rest of my life, that I don't think he understands exactly what I want to do [because he is not involved in the church]. Right now I would like to go to seminary and be a minister and there's times when I've felt he just doesn't understand that it's so important to me.... He thinks I can do anything that I want to do. I think in a way being a doctor and a lawyer or something big like that is more what he's always dreamed of having a daughter to be, and that's not what I'm doing.... I know I could be a good doctor if I wanted to or a good lawyer if I wanted to, but that's not want I want to do and it's not worth it."

The sadness Valerie felt in the absence of her father's affirmation and understanding of her particular vocational quest underscores the significance many of these girls attributed to parental blessings of their vocational yearnings, hopes, and aspirations. It mattered to them to share their hopes, dreams, and plans with parents who could bless their daughters with some understanding of what those plans meant to the girls.

Taking pride in their parents' work

Another way parents bless the vocational yearnings and struggles of their adolescent daughters is by engaging in work that their daughters respect, or at least by performing their work in a manner that their daughters value and respect. Jessica spoke admiringly of both her mother's and father's work, affirming not only the kind of professions in which each engages, but also the motivations she perceives them to have: "My mother is incredible. She is smart and beautiful and wonderful in dealing with people. Both my parents, their lives have been for unselfish reasons....I love that I can be proud of them and all they've done; I think that's really important. My mom works to put diversity in college curriculums, and she used to be a women's studies professor....My dad came from a really conservative background....And he ended up being a conscientious objector to Vietnam, which I think some people are like 'Oh those draft dodgers,' but I am *so* proud of that. I love that. I think that is awesome. It's something he really strongly believes in....I love that about my dad; I think that's really neat. And then he went working for peace and arms control....So my parents both do these really worthwhile important things."

As for her own vocational interests, Jessica said later in the interview, "You know, everybody here is talking about going to seminary, being priests whatever. I find that very interesting....If you're asking what I want to do with my life, I want to be able to do things that I know are right,...to look around and make sure I am doing something worthwhile. 'Cause that's part of what I mean when I say that's what I respect so much about my parents." In spite of the importance she placed upon her desire to use her life in worthwhile ways, Jessica did not appear to feel pressured toward making a preemptive decision about what to do with her life by prematurely deciding on a career track such as going to seminary. Instead, blessed with a framework for shaping a meaningful life that both parents modeled for her, Jessica was openly engaged in an ongoing search for her own particular ways to make a difference in the world.

Carol, reflecting on her mother's work in a care facility for disabled persons, spoke of the admiration she felt for her mother, who had moved from a starting job providing direct physical care for the residents there, to putting herself through school and becoming the director of personnel for the same nonprofit organization: "Throughout the years she has just stayed there because she likes her job....My mom is one of my heroes. I really admire her....I mean there are a lot of things about her I don't like, necessarily, but she and my grandma are both very giving. My mom doesn't get paid very much but she still works at her job because she likes the fact of what she's doing."

Carol was uncertain about the precise direction her own vocational path would take, but thought she might spend time after college in the Peace Corp like an aunt of hers: "I don't know if I want to make a living out of it like my aunt did, but I'd at least like to do that. I really think service is important. I know everyone has their own calling, but I think that for me, it's really in the area of service. I feel like everyone's responsible to help change systems of oppression or chaos, and I feel like the way I could help do that is through service."

These girls indicated that they were quite attentive to the kinds of work in which their parents engaged, to their parents' attitudes about their work, and to the amount of time parents spent at work. Interestingly, however, as a group the girls sometimes seemed not to know much about their parents' educational backgrounds. They often responded to questions about the type and amount of education their parents have with uncertainty, as if this topic had not been discussed with the girls in any detail. As one girl wrote, "I know she [my mother] went to school a lot, but I don't think she ever got any degrees. What kind of degree do you need to be an accountant? I know that's what she does, but I have no idea how she got there."

Girls in late adolescence are on the brink of decisions that will structure "how they get there" in terms of entry into the adult world of work. They operate with an understanding of vocation in which one's adult labors constitute an important part of how one uses time, talents, gifts, and abilities for God's mission of reconciling the world. Therefore, access to many different adult models of "how to get there," or the educational, networking, and other entry points into particular forms of work, becomes too important to leave to chance. The reason such models are so important, of course, is underscored by the examples in the preceding section, in which girls indicate how attentive they are to the meanings of the work in which their parents engage.

Parents informing girls' vocations
by negative experiences or examples

Of course, not all the girls with whom we spoke narrated such positive portraits of parental support in their lives. Many spoke of conflicts in their family relationships, of times of deep hurt or of abandonment or betrayal by a parent. Others at times spoke critically of parents' life choices and actions. We call this a *via negativa*, in which parents provide both motivation and substance to girls' vocational aspirations through negative experience or example.

One form such a *via negativa* took among the group of girls we interviewed involved parents acting as something or someone to struggle against, such that their daughters formed strong ideas of what they did *not* want to do or be like in their own lives and identities. A consistent theme throughout sixteen-year-old Kelly's interview, for instance, concerned her struggle to claim and maintain a sense of her unique value and worth as a young woman in the face of a history of abuse by her father. At the time of her interview, her position on the journey into young adult vocation was that of a person trying to claim a positive female identity — to be a person of value and worth who is also a woman — a position she occupied in part through her experiences of paternal messages to the contrary. Asked about the experience of being a girl in her family, Kelly replied, "I knew [my dad] didn't like girls. Because when my mom was pregnant with my sister, he kept saying, "Let's have a boy, we want a boy, a Smith boy." And like we didn't get a boy. . . . I knew he was like happy with who we are — he wouldn't like switch us for a boy. But I also knew that deep down inside, doesn't every dad want a boy, you know? But my mom was always telling me, 'No, he wanted girls. He kept telling me he wanted girls.' But I'll never forget that conversation with my dad."

She described a painful childhood in which she experienced many different ways of feeling devalued by her father. Out of this negative memory, and in conjunction with many girl-affirming messages received in her all-girls school and from her mother, whom she described as "an incredibly strong woman — I want to be like her,"

Kelly elsewhere expressed strong motivation to "find some way to make a difference, to love and to care. Women can do that well, you know."

Of the fifty girls I (Joyce) interviewed, twelve came from families in which their parents were divorced, separated, or never married with the daughter growing up in a single-parent household. It cannot be inferred on the basis of these interviews that the relationships between girls and their parents necessarily have more stress or less affection for one or both parents in situations of divorce than among families comprised of a married couple with children (where, according to the girls' reports, there was sometimes also a significant amount of stress and antipathy). In this group of interviews, however, we find multiple examples of girls for whom the breach of relationship between parents also represents a breach of relationship between one or both parents and their daughters.

In other instances, girls experienced emotional absence of a parent due to physical or mental illness, addiction, or educational or workplace demands. Several of these situations provide different examples of the *via negativa* through which girls engaged their own vocational struggles; girls described perspectives they embrace as a result of the difficulties they encountered with parents.

Cathy, a young woman from a working-class community, described herself as "really close" to her father as a young child. He was not involved in her life consistently, because he and her mother had never married, and then he died when she was nine years old: "He didn't want to be married and there were times when I don't think he wanted to be a father. . . . He just wanted to be a father when he felt like he needed to be a father. And so that was good for him but I don't know if that was the best thing for us, because we didn't always have a man in the home. Our concept was, Dad, well when he gets here then he's a dad."

When Cathy talked about her future plans and sense of purpose, what came through repeatedly was the high value she placed on people "taking responsibility, carrying their share of the load," a value at least partially forged in response to the parenting she received. For example, Cathy named as her response to the presence of suffering in the world that she would "ask what the world is coming to and ask God how she can help." She offered as a general sense of purpose "the ability to make a difference in people, the world, my church and community."

At the same time, however, financial independence had a key place in her statements about what was most significant both for her own future and for the present (she had a part-time job that was very important to her). "Financially, my mom has never been, like, she's never made enough money to get everything we always needed, let alone everything she's wanted. And so that really changed my life in that I have this deep love and yearn[ing] for money. It sounds funny, but it was definitely a financial struggle." As Cathy reflected further on the painful aspects of her family situation and the loss of her father, she commented, "It's made me a stronger person, because it kind of breaks the role that a girl always needs a man, or that a girl always needs her father, and it's made my mom a stronger person too and not so dependent on other people, and it showed me self-reliance and not always having to rely on somebody else for everything."

While it is possible to hear a certain defensiveness in Cathy's comments about the independence she values (e.g., a determination not to need anyone as a protection against future rejection), there is also evidence of a hard-won strength, the ability to face adversity and come out of it intact. Cathy, seeing herself as someone who has become strong through having to deal with such personal difficulties, wants to turn that personal strength toward others who might benefit from it, by finding ways she can use her experiences for good. Asked how she would like to be remembered, she offered this "epitaph" for herself: "She loved, lived, and worked for God and others."

What is important about these examples is *not* that they somehow demonstrate that even bad things turn out all right for these girls, or other such false platitudes. Rather, these difficult experiences underscore the remarkable resilience of these girls. The girls show an amazing ability to mobilize the symbols and stories of their faith as resources in making meaning of such difficult and painful life experiences. The result is hopeful reflections about the meanings and purposes of their lives — in short, their present and future senses of vocation.

Of course, the meanings they made were not always positive and happy. For example, some girls like Cathy parented by single mothers described watching their mothers' financial stress and difficulties with sole responsibility for work in the labor force and in the home. These experiences seemed to have bequeathed to these girls a certain sense of "drivenness" to avoid the ending up in the same situation as their mothers. Such factors, too, become important aspects of their quests toward meaningful vocations in the world.

Finding a new empathy for parents

In several of our conversations with young women, the girls stood at an empathic turning point in relation to their parents, as they seemed to reconsider earlier judgments made of their parents in a new light. Girls spoke of formerly being critical of choices their parents made, often based upon the negative consequences such choices had had for the girls. For instance, Carol, describing her feelings toward her mother who "always has to work late," said that earlier in her teen years "we didn't always get along that well. I was resentful of her, probably unfairly, because we never had the 'normal' family life. . . . I don't feel resentful toward her anymore, because I know that it's not her fault. I mean, she didn't have any other choice. And I guess when I was littler, I didn't understand the seriousness of it. But now [I see that] just to keep a roof over our heads, food, clothes, all that stuff, she *had* to do that. It wasn't like a choice she made, so I don't feel like that toward her anymore."

Carol spoke of feeling greater compassion for her divorced, single-parent mother, of recently becoming more sympathetic to her mother's situation and being able to see her mother as a person who faced serious dilemmas. Several girls echoed this perspective. Whereas earlier

Carol had thought about her mother's long work hours and her parent's decision to end their marriage mainly in terms of the negative impact upon her (Carol), at the time of the interview she was reassessing those earlier judgments. It seems as if a certain rapprochement was taking place for Carol and other girls who at age seventeen could grant their parents an interior life of their own, and also became willing to grant that at least sometimes their parents' choices may have been the best ones they could have made under the circumstances.

Lauri, whose mother had suffered from a debilitating neurological illness since Lauri was a young child, described recently coming to terms with her mother's condition and her own interpretations of it: "I've just now started to become close to her, because her disease started progressing when I was young. And at the time I felt like she was just trying to avoid me, or that she really didn't love me, because she couldn't take me places or do stuff with me. But I realize now that it was just her disease, it was not her fault at all. But it still hurt when I was little because I didn't realize that. But now we're starting to grow closer together." Like Carol's reflections on her new relationship with her mother, Lauri's comments show a change in the capacity to see her mother on her mother's own terms rather than only as she exists in the experience of the daughter.

In both instances, these girls' re-evaluation of their earlier critical stances suggests a more complex cognitive capacity at work (one that allows a more nuanced construction of the interiority of another person) but also a deepening emotional capacity as well (one that allows the extension of empathy even amid the experience of personal pain from the person toward whom empathy is directed).

As such, it appears characteristic of most of the girls in this group that in late adolescence they came to understand and accept some of the choices made by their parents, choices of which they had been highly critical or by which they merely felt victimized in earlier adolescence. In many of these interviews girls described parental decisions or choices generating conflict in parent-daughter relationships — choices and decisions such as divorce, imposing limits on spending in their households, or the need to devote time to work that took time away from direct parent involvement with their daughters. And frequently, the girls go on to express a new empathy and understanding for their parents.

Of course, one of the risks of these deepening capacities for empathy to which young women may be particularly subject is the risk of unhealthy codependence if girls take on the role of caretaker of the parent with whom they empathically identify or for whom they may feel responsibility. Beth, whose family experience included one parent's illness resulting in the other parent's decision to return to school full time in order to have better work to support herself and her children, found herself the caretaker and de facto parent of younger siblings: "I was always home with my little brother. If he was sick, he would call on me. And so it was like my mom was depending on me too because she was trying to be strong but there was just no way, she was just falling apart."

Beth's vocational aspirations include a legal career, possibly getting involved in national politics. However, she reports a complete lack of interest in "being married or having kids, I don't want to do any of that stuff." It is not difficult to surmise that from her current vantage point, she has already been in a parenting role and fears the problems that arise from close relationships. Her life experiences discourage her from seeing relationships with a spouse, partner, or children as an aspect of her vocation that can coexist alongside her professional goals.

Rona is a young woman whose parents emigrated to the United States from the Philippines. For her, this late adolescent time of revisiting earlier critiques of parents took shape in terms of Rona's insertion of a particular Filipino cultural value into her interpretation of her family relationships. *Utang na loob*, the "debt of gratitude" owed to one's family or others, describes an intense relationship of being bound to others by gratitude. This debt of gratitude takes place in a cultural context that tends to put the well-being of kin or community ahead of one's own personal gain. In Rona's case, she described her family giving up their homeland and preferred life in the Philippines to being in the U.S. so that she and her siblings might have more opportunities for education and growth.[4]

She reflects on this sacrifice of theirs, as a result of which she experiences a "debt of gratitude":

> *My father will say, "Oh, I'm going to go back to the Philippines, it's so much easier there." He's from farming country.... You live with your family. You have everything within the community. Here it's so much harder. There's discrimination. You have to know how to do so many things, like work on the computer.... Sometimes I feel bad for them, because they work really hard and they don't have as much as other people who are born here.... My father got laid off, so now it's pretty much just been my mother. So my mom, I hate her for this, she goes and works there over the weekend. So I don't really have time to see her anymore. [And she does that because] college is coming up for me, and I don't have money. But they want me to go to a good school [crying].... Sometimes when I think about college, I really want to go away and have new experiences, things like that. But at the same time, that's kind of four years away from the parents who you didn't really get to know, at least not for my father.... Well, I know my mom has become more of a friend.... In some ways our relationships have gotten more open, because of things, because I've become more open.*

In this reappraisal of the choices her parents made about work and where to live, Rona's former, straightforward critique that she disapproved of her mother's long working hours now appears somewhat moderated by Rona's more multidimensional awareness that the

---

4. We are reporting on Rona's perceptions here, and not asserting a perspective of United States culture and society as necessarily providing superior opportunities for children's education and growth. The material affluence of North America in contrast to the extreme poverty in much of the Philippines lends a concrete dimension to the perspective that parents can procure more resources for their children in the United States. Unfortunately this concrete reality can easily collude with a cultural imperialism that we reject.

very thing she criticized has been done on behalf of her future educational opportunities. As Rona shifted her understanding from a too simple rejection of her parents' life choices as bad for her, to a recognition of the tradeoffs involved in such choices, her parents began to appear less two-dimensional in her depictions of them. Rona's previous assessments of her parents as "really traditional" and as bound by culture appeared to be shifting as well, as she discovered her own sense of gratitude to them for the future they hoped to help lay before her.

How does such a late adolescent "rapprochement" relate to parental blessings of the vocational struggles of adolescent girls? First, when girls who have engaged primarily in critique of their parents now "make their peace" with them, they demonstrate an important cognitive shift. These girls are involved in a more complex pattern of thinking. They are able to hold together multiple dimensions about the life-choices of others that allow them to see these others with greater compassion and empathy.

At the same time that they are able to see that the choices and decisions of parents seldom have been unambiguous, these girls are also in touch with the ambiguity of their own decision making and vocational struggles: whether to choose a college major they feel passionate about or one that will give them access to a lucrative job; how to balance the desires for love, romance, and companionship with the desires for meaningful work in the world as they sometimes make decisions to leave a relationship in order to pursue a particular educational path. Able to recognize and grapple with complexity in their own choice making, these girls also bring new understanding to the choice making of others, including parents.

In effect, the girls may gain a new companion on their vocational journeys — Rona and Carol both spoke of becoming more like friends with their mothers, being able to share more and be more open. Gilligan and Rogers's work on mother-daughter relationships in adolescence suggests that such capacities for deeper empathy and understanding reflect cognitive and emotional growth among girls that "make possible a different kind of relationship between mother and daughter, in part because the daughter is better able to feel and see into her mother's life."[5] In the quest toward meaning and purposeful work in the world, such deep relational connections form a potentially vital part of the network of mentoring and modeling adults who help to apprentice adolescent girls into young adult vocations worthy of their efforts and dreams.

Second, while such rapprochement appears neither automatic nor without its own conflicts and difficulties, it can represent a reciprocal experience of the Christian practice of forgiving others and being forgiven by others, a practice that brings a realistic moderation to what might otherwise turn vocational passion into a false sense of invincibility and a concomitant false sense of self. Various theorists addressing women's vocational achievement and development have named the "imposter syndrome" as a common experience of many women who make their way into educational and work positions to which they aspired, only to struggle against the constant fear of being discovered as an imposter who does not really belong there.[6]

The Christian practice of forgiveness may offer some inoculation against the imposter syndrome. In renegotiating their relationships with mothers, these girls in late adolescence practice both the art of recognizing and forgiving the shortcomings of another — even in cases where they experienced harm — as well as the experience of being forgiven, loved, and accepted in the face of their own shortcomings.

5. Carol Gilligan and Annie Rogers, "Reframing Daughtering and Mothering: Paradigm Shift in Psychology," in *Daughtering and Mothering: Female Subjectivity Reanalyzed,*ed. Janneke Van Mens-Verhulst, Karlein Schreurs, and Liesveth Woertman, (New York: Rutledge, 1993), 125–34.

6. For two recent treatments of this concept in psychology and education respectively, see J. J. Kolligian and R. J. Sternberg, "Perceived Fraudulence in Young Adults: Is There an 'Imposter Syndrome'?" *Journal of Personality Assessment* 56, no. 2 (1991): 308–26, and F. M. Reis, "Internal Barriers, Personal Issues, and Decisions Faced by Gifted and Talented Females," *Gifted Child Today* 25, no. 1 (2000): 14–28. In addition, many thinkers across disciplines draw on the work of Alice Miller, *The Drama of the Gifted Child: The Search for the True Self* (New York: Basic Books, 1997), to address the roots of this issue in the experience of both women and men.

A perspective on parenting, youth ministry, and adolescent girls

Until the 1980s one of the dominant understandings of adolescence viewed the primary developmental task of teenagers as that of separation from parents toward establishing their own identities. Accordingly, the related task of parenting in the teen years involved mothers and fathers in providing the parental counterpart to this separation and identity formation — either by "lovingly letting go" of their separating teens or by providing targets for adolescent rebellion and opposition so that such separation might be accomplished. Feminist practitioners and scholars challenged this framework, particularly in relation to the experiences of adolescent girls. As a result, a variety of alternative perspectives on parenting adolescent girls emerged that emphasize adolescence as a time of *the renegotiation of relationships* between girls and their parents, rather than focused on separation.

That is, fathers, mothers, and daughters together are involved in the business of "updating" their relationships, transforming their ways of being connected, and constructing these relationships in new ways in relation to the transformations undergone by both adolescents and their parents. Rather than viewing conflict between girls and their parents as some kind of necessary "storm and stress" of adolescent development, it is possible to view the movements of conflict and rapprochement in these relationships as constituting diverse patterns of renegotiating what closeness and space will mean for this new time of life.

What girls said about their parents in interviews affirms this idea that during adolescence, girls work out different forms of connection with their parents from those held during childhood. Adolescence is therefore a time to update family relationships to fit the new capacities and life situations of all the family members.

Implications for youth ministry are numerous. First, if current efforts emphasizing youth ministry as family ministry succeed in turning youth ministry toward addressing parents along with young people, these conversations with girls underscore an important focus of such efforts: namely, helping parents become more conscious of their power to bless the vocational strivings of their daughters. Some parents may not know how important it is for them to "believe in their daughters out loud."

Sometimes, because of particular experiences and histories within families, adolescent daughters may not know how to hear or receive such affirmations from their own parents. Parents may not be aware of the significance of their own work and life choices for the vocational quests of their daughters and may not have shared their stories of education and other preparation for how they live meaningful lives. They may be so caught up in anxieties about the material security and well-being of their children that they fail to address other aspects of the meanings of love and work. Or sometimes parents may not have a Christian theological perspective on their own gifts and work. This is a proposal for youth ministry to be a space in which parents and youth alike find resources and opportunities for practicing their lives as a calling from God.

Young women on vocational journeys need mentors and companions in crafting lives of passionate engagement, advocacy, and responsibility to others through which they may find purpose and meaning without requiring them to vacate their own personhood. The young women who have been our guides in these conversations on vocation make clear that they understand Christian vocation in terms of making a difference in the world, addressing oppression and injustice, and giving one's self in service to something and someone greater than one's self alone. When youth ministry continues to focus itself around "private practices" of entertainment, of teaching young people what to believe instead of how to believe, and of treating the life of faith as some sort of personal morality play instead of a radical calling to walk in the way of Jesus, then youth ministry misses its central calling and opportunity to engage young people in the public practices and mission that are the Christian faith.

At the same time, we know that young women are frequently invited into forms of service that require them to divest their own selfhood in acts of codependence. In spite of important gains made toward women's equality, ours is a world that still encourages women to serve and men to receive service. Consequently, there is need for a youth ministry that blatantly resists such injustices. This is a proposal for a mission-centered, practice-oriented youth ministry that takes a sophisticated approach to gender differences among youth in the meanings and practices of mission for others.

Second, these young women's stories of renegotiating relationships with parents indicate both the rich satisfaction but also the damaging pain that girls can experience in their families. Too often youth ministry holds up an idealized vision of family life that bears little resemblance to the multifaceted families from which these and other girls come. And instead of offering youth the most experienced pastoral care resources in the church, those charged with caring for youth and assisting them through this potentially fragile renegotiation are often novices in those aspects of ministry concerned with the arts of Christian care and counseling.

In the relatively small number of interviews represented in the research for this book, girls described major impediments to their spiritual, physical, and emotional well-being that they experience within their family contexts — everything from their inabilities to forgive fathers for affairs or mothers for decisions to divorce, to questions about their value and worth as females, to depression suffered by one or more family members. These girls held on to untold stories of past abuse or betrayal that they knew created present-tense problems for them in relationships in and beyond their families. They suffered from the inevitable conflicts between their own needs and those of their all-too-human parents. In particular, these conversations with girls underscore the need for much more pastoral attention to young women's experiences of grief and loss. This is a proposal for youth ministry to be a space for focused theological reflection on complex family relationships; for youth ministry that offers skilled pastoral care with youth as they attempt to deal with family realities; and for youth ministry as a place of encounter between young women and other (non-parental) adults who can share in the responsibility for their thriving and who can mentor them in ever-deepening, more "adult" ways of practicing Christian faith.

Last, the separation of youth ministry from the rest of the church's mission and ministries often means that youth ministry operates as if in a parallel universe, separated from the issues and concerns of the church as a whole. The wider church could learn a great deal about vocation as the theological quest to align individual and communal life with the mission and purposes of God for the world, by participating in the vocational struggles of youth. The girls represented in this chapter spoke as Christians who know that their faith does and will matter for the life of the world, however intangible their current sense of direction might be.

Clearly, there are many important ways for parents to support the religious lives of their adolescent daughters by supporting their vocational struggles and questions. And the church can be a place that upholds both parents and youth in such efforts, with its distinctively theological construal of the meanings and purposes of human life. In turn, young women can and will contribute to the renewal of the church's understandings of its own vocation. This, then, is a proposal for youth ministry to resist the tendency to operate as a separate entity from the rest of the church, and instead to allow the vocational struggles of young women to be a part of the wider church's search for its identity and purposes in the life of God. It is also a call to understand young women through the eyes of Julie's self understanding, as being "like Job's daughters" — women who go out into the world named and equipped with a vocational and spiritual inheritance from their parents and the church, so that they might make a difference.

There's more to this story

Culturally shaped gender roles have had a significant, limiting effect on the vocational options available to girls and women (not only in terms of work but also other arenas of vocational expression such as participation in religious communities and family roles).

And yet young women are not the only ones who must address issues of gender as they seek ways to offer their lives vocationally. For boys, too, gender identity intersects with vocation as young men face the challenges of finding a vocational path to walk amid changing male gender norms. The next chapter looks at these issues. In it, we propose an adaptation of a method of story theology (initially developed by Dori for use with girls and introduced in the last chapter as a way of reflecting on film) as a way of inviting young men to articulate their stories of vocation.

Chapter 7

Isaac's long walk

Keeping faith with guys on the path to wholeness

Jay, who is in seminary to become a religious educator, remembers encountering sexist attitudes from trusted authorities while negotiating his career path. "My pastor pretty blatantly told me that anything short of ordained ministry was not a status job, especially for a man," Jay recalls. In a world where girls can supposedly be anything, boys are often steered away from work in caring professions, which traditionally have lower status and lower pay. Although we typically think of sexism as having a negative effect only on girls and women, here we see how all of humanity can be diminished by cultural stereotypes of gender. If Jay succumbs to the voices directing him toward higher status and pay, he may spend years of his life chasing a carrot he never gets to enjoy.

Luckily for Jay, there were other voices affirming the match between his demonstrated gifts as a teacher, reflective Christian, mission leader, and attentive friend — all of which coalesce nicely with his current job as a youth minister. "When I told my dad that I had decided to become a professional church educator, he just smiled and said, 'Well, son, isn't that what you always wanted to be?'" Jay expresses gratitude that his father was able to bestow this blessing, just months before dying of cancer. The blessing provided support to the dubious project of following one's inner voice, despite strong signals that could thwart an authentic call. In the last chapter, we looked at parents, vocation, and adolescent girls. Here we turn toward adolescent boys. We do this with a bit of hesitation. We are women who have devoted our energies to the thriving of girls in a still-patriarchal world.

We are all too aware that we cannot speak for boys or men. Nor can we be insiders to male experience. As invested outsiders, who care about boys and men in many capacities, we do however notice and want to attend to some of the particularities we see there. In this era of shifting gender roles and wider possibilities for girls' vocational expression, many people wonder, "What about our boys?" What are the unique needs and capacities of boys, and where are they being unheard or under-tended?[1] We explore the broad spectrum of psychological literature dealing with adolescent boys of varying races, classes, and ethnicities. We set those findings in conversation with one promising method of evoking boys' stories and broadening boys' emotional repertoires. And we wonder about other ways the church might explicitly support new narratives, stories in which boys and men are constructing their identities in a world that no longer strictly determines what masculinity looks like.

In experiencing a father who supported his countercultural career choice, Jay likens himself to Isaac, a young man who took a long walk with his dad to an unknown destination (Genesis 23). Unaware of Abraham's intention, Isaac follows trustingly in his father's footsteps. Although Abraham ventures quite close to making an enormous sacrifice, in the end, he proved faithful to both his son and his God. Jay hears resonance between his own father and the biblical father Abraham, who stayed open to God's unfolding plan, despite a host of embedded messages telling him what culture would advise.

Even in its troublesome beginning, the story of Abraham's call to sacrifice his son lifts up themes we recognize in our own lives as parents, mentors, and guides. Destinations beckon to us. Sometimes we fail to sufficiently question the enormity of the sacrifices we make to financial success, high status, and purported job security. Blinded perhaps by implicit motives, we adults bring our youth along on this journey, training them without words to gravitate toward certain markers of the well-lived life. These unexamined journeys can

1. See Robert Dykstra, with Allan Cole and Donald Capps, *The Spirituality of Adolescent Boys: Losers, Loners and Rebels* (Louisville: Westminster John Knox Press, 2007).

exact undue sacrifice. They can demand that a young person give up part or all of themselves.

We notice such hard sacrifices quite literally in the return of wounded soldiers from Iraq, fitted with prosthetics to replace limbs blown away by hand-made bombs. More enormous still is the sacrifice of those soldiers who do not return. We see the sacrifice of male wholeness more figuratively when we consider the disproportionate ratio of males incarcerated in our nation's prisons and the specter of male-on-female violence played out in dating and domestic spheres.[2] When we acknowledge that suicide is the third leading cause of death for boys fifteen to twenty four years of age, we must admit our boys are suffering.[3] While women also suffer prominently in all of these instances, a significant loss accrues for men.

Poor and minority boys surely face starker losses in a racist and classist society. An African American mother told about a sad moment in her mothering life when her bright prepubescent son announced that "he was no longer cute and cuddly" in the eyes of the world. He had clearly soaked in the racist message that young black men are to be feared. This mother expressed the concern that all the good mothering in the world could not make up for the stark reality of internalized racism. A Korean man involved in the study of youth ministry expressed the flip side of the "perfect minority" stereotype of Asian American immigrants. Despite family support that encourages educational success, Asian American adolescent boys often experience great difficulty forming identity in the cross-fire between their parent's expectations and the vicissitudes of high school worlds.

White men and men from upper- and upper-middle-class status are also bringing to voice the ache of lives unfulfilled. As one white, middle-class woman recently remarked about her young adult son, "He knows the way it's supposed to work — college, career, family — but it's just not turning out that way for him, and he reads this as a failure." Her friend responded "My husband followed all the rules,

---

2. *www.cdc.gov/ncipc/factsheets/ipvfacts.htm*, Access date, 12/04/06.
3. *www.cdc.gov/ncipc/factsheets/suifacts.htm*, Access date, 12/04/06.

and now at midlife, looks around to see all of the pieces of himself he left behind along the way while climbing a corporate ladder."

Clearly, as we look around at boys becoming men in our midst, there is reason for alarm and concern, calling for disciplined reflection on the causes to which boys are sacrificed and the possible remedies youth ministry might offer.

Boys showing up on our radar

As mothers of daughters and theological educators who have dedicated much of our professional lives to thinking about the religious needs of young women, we entered this boys' world determined to resist the gendered stereotypes of which we knew to be suspicious. We also hesitated to notice too carefully the literature on boys' poor academic performance, because so often this conversation cloaks a reaction against feminist gains. Despite these hesitations, boys kept showing up on our radar. Individually, we reflect on these experiences.

First, Dori, who is raising two daughters, reflects on finding herself teaching a mostly boys' Sunday school class and befriending mothers of sons:

At first, boys' worlds seemed alien and uncomfortable. I didn't know how to get boys to talk, to open up, to trust, and to share — key components for me of any good Bible study or Sunday school lesson. The boys were, however, quite ready for action. They wanted to move, to bounce, and to wrap themselves up in my crazy quilt so as to better wriggle all over the smooth tile floor of the classroom. Given wriggle time, I soon realized, boys held the capacity for deep introspection and had plenty of wisdom to share, often humorously. The key, I learned from intuition and fly-by-the-seat-of-my-pants improvisation, was to re-imagine learning spaces that embraced body, mind, and spirit simultaneously.

A mother of a son once implored me: "I know where to go to get good books to inspire my daughter to be smart, strong, and bold, but who's publishing books on boy's self-esteem?" While my first reaction was to reply that almost the entire canon of Western literature reflects the male experience, my kinder, gentler side emerged, remembering that contemporary parents have been trained to seek manageable, packaged resources for life's troubling quandaries. I quickly provided her with a bibliography.[4]

Here Joyce, who is raising twin boys in addition to a daughter, reflects on the naïveté of her pre-boy existence:

I was determined to avoid the pitfalls of gendered "shoulds" in raising boys. This would include such tactics as rejecting an urge to guide my boys away from their emotions during a squabble on the playground and encouraging them to choose from a wide-range of toys, including dolls. We don't buy toy guns in our home, for instance, and yet — as just about any parent of boys will testify — our boys managed to make guns anyway, from sticks, pencils, any available item.[5] But I grew to revisit some of my hard-won beliefs about culture's influence on gendered behaviors. I was a complete believer in the social construction of gender (almost to the exclusion of any role for biology) before I had boys. Then I realized that some of what I saw in them was "hard-wired" — they have been, from the beginning, shaped by a complex web of culture and biology. I have come to understand that culture and biology are always mutual forces. These forces shape identity and behavior simultaneously, in an ongoing feedback loop that defies our tendency to see either culture or biology as primary.[6]

---

4. Michael Gurian, *What Stories Does My Son Need? Books and Movies that Build Character in Boys* (New York: Putnam, 2000). This is a good start. It provides a bibliography of books and movies, listed by age-appropriateness.

5. We are acutely aware of the lures that recruit boys into the words and images of war. Researchers note the link between video games marketed to boys and de-sensitization to graphic depictions of violence on and off-screen (Nick Turse, "Bringing the War Home: The New Military-Industrial-Entertainment Complex at War and Play," *www.commondreams.org*, October 17, 2993) Especially during the era of the U.S. war with Iraq, it is difficult to ignore the ways in which the newest re-lease of games for the X-box trains boys to be soldiers in a much more sophisticated way than the GI-Joes of past generations.

6. Barbara Rogoff, a cultural psychologist whose studies across cultures focus on the intersections of culture and human development, rejects the notion that there

In addition to these seemingly hard-wired differences, boys also constantly breathe in societal messages about what boy-identity should be. Among these pressures and societal messages are ones that shape boy's attitudes to look down on girls. These perspectives construct male identity as superior by virtue of female identity being inferior. It seems that in spite of my best parenting efforts, my sons get a heavy dose of this perspective. One day, for example, one of my sons came home announcing that a classmate had been beaten in arm wrestling "by a girl, and that's really bad if even a girl can beat you!"

•

Together, as we've watched the boys we know move through late elementary school and into middle school and beyond, we've found ourselves fretting in parental tones. Why are so many boys being diagnosed with Attention Deficit Disorder, treated with Ritalin, and showing up in the principal's office to be disciplined for disrupting the classroom? Why is the elementary school so clearly designed with small-motor skills — which develop later in boys — in mind? When do boys — many of them scheduled from breakfast at school straight through until dinnertime childcare pickup — get to really open up and release the energy with which they seemed to be frothing? No wonder they didn't want to come to church on Sunday morning to complete yet another word maze and sit still for yet another info-drop! At times, it makes us wonder, in tones reminiscent of John Westerhoff's classic work on socialization in religious education, "Will our *boys* have faith?"[7]

Our scholarly activism had been engaged in the late 1980s around research that showed clear disadvantages for girls in education, primarily in math and science. In addition to this, we learned that early

---

exists an underlying, precultural human (generally identified with the biological), which culture then comes to "influence." As Rogoff puts it, "Human beings are biologically cultural" (Barbara Rogoff, *The Cultural Nature of Human Development* [New York: Oxford University Press, 2003], 63).

7. John Westerhoff, *Will Our Children Have Faith,* rev. ed. (Harrisburg, Pa.: Morehouse, 2000, 1976).

adolescence is a time when girls' social, emotional, and spiritual health often takes a precipitous dive. As noted in the previous chapter, the works of Carol Gilligan, Lyn Mikel Brown, Mary Pipher, and others convinced a growing number of us working in the discipline of religious education to take seriously this psychological research in our attempts to craft healing spaces of spiritual formation for girls.

Much of Dori's vocational expression came to focus around enlarging a vision of church in which girls' voices could be honored, particularly through acts of naming of God from the images of their own lives, as they reflected the body of women's history and storytelling. Joyce turned toward exploring "girltalk" on faith and families, a study of the ways girls make sense of being Christian and female today, and how their families support their religious lives.[8] As Dori published *Doing Girlfriend Theology: God-Talk with Young Women* and began providing workshops and consultations for local churches and denominational gatherings around issues pertinent to girls and women's development, she began to repeatedly hear participants voice the concern: How does this method of religious education speak to boys' unique needs? Knowing that churches have such a long history of male-dominated leadership did not diffuse a nagging awareness that somehow boys needed something from church that they weren't getting.

Beyond the boy code: Boy cultures as diverse and multilayered

And so we turned our attention to the psychological welfare of boys. A flurry of best-selling books urged parents and professionals to "rescue and protect" boys. These books raised awareness of the issues related to the spiritual, emotional, and social development of boys. They describe a "boy code" that encourages bravado at the expense of emotional attachment and a "gender straitjacket" that limits boys'

---

8. Joyce Ann Mercer, *GirlTalk on Faith and Families* (working title) (San Francisco: Jossey-Bass, forthcoming).

ability to express themselves freely.[9] The boy code can be summarized to encompass four stereotypes of male ideals: that males should be independent, strong, and stoic; that males are naturally macho and full of bravado; that males want to achieve power and status and, simultaneously, avoid shame; and that males do not express thoughts, feelings, or ideals that are deemed feminine including dependence, warmth, and empathy.[10]

This body of boy-literature, sociologist Michael Kimmel points out, is limited because it largely reflects white middle- and upper-middle-class boys' experiences. Generalizing from this cohort to *all* boys obscures more than it points out, Kimmel writes in the foreword to *Adolescent Boys: Exploring Diverse Cultures of Boyhood*.[11] While not diminishing the relevance of the boy code and the limits it places on boys constructing identities, Kimmel critiques this body of literature for all it omits:

> What was missing, then, were all the "other" boys — African American boys, Latino boys, Asian American boys, working-class boys, boys from countries other than the United States. Also missing were gay boys, bisexual boys, boys who didn't yet know their sexual orientation.... But these boys also contend with the boy code — and they do so in different ways, with different social, cultural, and economic resources, as these boys find their way toward manhood.[12]

---

9. William Pollack, *Real Boys: Rescuing Our Sons from the Myths of Boyhood* (New York: Random House, 1998); Daniel J. Kindlon and Michael Thompson, *Raising Cain* (New York: Ballantine, 1999); William Pollack, *Real Boys' Voices* (New York: Random House, 2000); Michael Gurian, *The Wonder of Boys: What Parents, Mentors, and Educators Can Do to Shape Boys into Exceptional Men* (New York: Putnam, 1997); Michael Gurian, *The Good Son: Shaping the Moral Development of Our Boys and Young Men* (New York: Penguin, 1999); Michael Gurian, *The Minds of Boys: Saving Our Sons from Falling Behind in School and Life* (San Francisco: Jossey-Bass, 2005)

10. Pollack, *Real Boys,* 23–24.

11. Michael Kimmel, in the Foreword to *Adolescent Boys: Exploring Diverse Cultures of Boyhood,* ed. Niobe Way and Judy Y. Chu (New York: New York University Press, 2005), xii.

12. Ibid.

An additional critique of the literature is its tendency to blame feminists for problematizing "normal, rambunctious" boyhood and to set girls' gains over against boys' losses. Eugene Roehlkepartain, of the Search Institute, addresses this concern, writing that "boys aren't in their current situation because we've paid too much attention to girls. Indeed, one can argue that we haven't paid enough attention to either boys or girls."[13] Despite the emphasis on opportunities for girls in recent decades, there is still much to be done. Roehlkepartain cites a 2000 study by the Washington, D.C.-based Public Education Network (www.publiceducation.org/) that found "a dearth of opportunities for young women.... We found both an absolute level of underservice to girls overall in communities, and too many instances of girls being treated as second-class citizens in coeducational programs," the study reported.

Kimmel argues that if we want to help boys — including white middle-class boys — we must listen to the voices of marginalized young males. These are the boys who, because of one minority status or another, feel most crushingly the difficulties of negotiating an acceptable masculinity. These are boys who are not passive recipients of a given masculine role: they are actively constructing their identities by rejecting, parodying, or accepting such stereotypes as the white male jock, the Asian-American perfect immigrant, the urban black male who is automatically assumed to be a gang member, or the high-maintenance metrosexual (a recent term coined to describe urban males who spend a great deal of time and money on their image and appearance). These diverse voices "open doors for the rest of us: doors of resilience and resistance to those very dominant norms," Kimmel writes.

Adolescent Boys, edited by Niobe Way and Judy Y. Chu, takes seriously boys of differing cultural contexts. This research follows in form and focus the work of early feminist scholars, who first studied middle-class white girls, and later discovered a richer tableau of

---

13. Eugene C. Roehlkepartain, *Connecting with Boys, Assets: The Magazine of Ideas for Healthy Communities and Healthy Youth*, Summer 2001, *www.search-institute.org/*.

experience when participant observers took time to listen carefully to girls who are poor, working-class, and of diverse ethnic origin. This wider picture of boys' development includes not just the clinical populations that tend to pathologize boy's behavior. We find here depictions of Hmong boys in Wisconsin making their way through high schools steeped in norms of white culture. We see depictions of adolescent black males, one in five of whom interviewed expressed suicidal ideation, and the importance of supportive fathers in preventing this risk. We read about Chinese boys' family dynamics and the importance of intimacy and male friendships in a cohort of urban boys of all races.

When open to these diverse cultural experiences, we can begin to imagine creative and life-giving responses from the resources of Christian tradition. These responses balance the possibility of interventions aimed at loosening the boy code, while remaining vigilant about practicing disciplined listening to *all* boys and the different ways they interact with the various cultures shaping them.

In crafting these responses from the resources of youth ministry, we have found particularly helpful one of the first of the boy bestsellers, *Raising Cain: Protecting the Emotional Lives of Boys,* by Dan Kindlon and Michael Thompson. Echoed in the work of psychologist William Pollack, these authors illumine a "culture of cruelty" in which boys enact a code of "manliness" involving dominance, fear, and betrayal. In the midst of this culture of cruelty and culturally defined norms of masculinity, significant losses occur. Primarily, boys lose trust, empathy, and relationship — key components of a healthy self image and the ability to share intimately with others.[14] This literature reveals that many boys are not adequately encouraged to develop a robust emotional repertoire. "We believe that boys, beginning at a young age, are systematically steered away from their emotional lives toward silence, solitude and distrust," the authors write.[15] Far from being the fault of individual mothers and fathers, the problem rests in

14. Kindlon and Thompson, *Raising Cain.*
15. Ibid.

a host of cultural norms defining gender assumptions which are often shaped and enacted from before birth on through early childhood and into adulthood.

When we began including *Raising Cain* as optional reading in youth ministry courses, male students — representing Caucasian middle-class, African exchange students, and Korean immigrants to America — were freed to put into words and images they had heretofore been unable to name. They grieved the losses boyhood had exacted, and began to see that masculinity was not a given, but had been constructed in a confluence of culture and biology. Women who read the book similarly voiced knowledge gained from encounters with males as parents, sons, pastors, friends, husbands, and lovers. Resoundingly, they framed the question: What can communities of faith offer to help boys lead more fulfilling lives?

In all of this work, the authors mention the spiritual lives of boys as deserving more attention. The resources of religion promise potential interventions that can counter cruelty and emotional detachment, providing safe spaces where boys can practice healthy ways of being human. Holding in tension the perspectives of both camps — the best-sellers and those attending to more diverse boys' experiences — allows a picture of boy-friendly churches and youth groups to emerge.

Roehlkepartain outlines what such boy-friendly spaces might look like, working out of the framework of developmental assets — a helpful model his research institute has detailed to assist organizations in fostering healthy emotional, spiritual, and social lives in young people. Providing guidelines to assist parents, church leaders, and teachers to better encourage boys' flourishing, he counsels us to:

- Offer alternatives to common stereotypes, thereby encouraging boys to explore more dimensions of themselves. This might mean recruiting volunteers and mentors who act in ways that are both strong *and* emotional, driven *and* contemplative.

- Move beyond one-size-fits-all thinking, tailoring our interactions to the individual needs of each young person. This might include offering small groups for boys and girls in which they are free to share their experiences of gendered-reality with one another and with caring adults who can provide positive role models.

- Tap boys' interests. Internalization of the boy code may lead some boys to shy away from activities that emphasize inward reflection. Some boys may need to be engaged through physical or intellectual challenge, which can set the stage for later moves toward introspection and meaning-making.

- Avoid sensationalizing boys' problems by focusing on the few dreadful incidents, such as school shootings and date rapes reported in the media. Remembering that the majority of boys are following less harmful paths toward adulthood helps avoid a crisis mentality implying that all boys are problems, rather than resources and gifts.

- Refuse to pit boys against girls, creating strict dichotomies that essentialize gender differences. This kind of thinking tends to make gender differences proscriptive, rather than simply descriptive. It is important to find ways to affirm the gifts and differences between us, not naming one way of being as inherently more god-like or ideal.[16]

These guidelines provide a useful starting place for moving the public debate beyond bully prevention curricula that have been successfully implemented in schools, churches, and community organizations. It helps us frame a question that can guide us to the theological issue: How might churches better provide boys with sufficient access to faith-partners and wisdom-guides, men and women who hold out for them the possibility of meaningful lives of work, family life, leisure, and volunteerism that frame their individual stories as part

16. Eugene C. Roehlkepartain, "Connecting with Boys: Closing the Asset Gap," *Assets: The Magazine of Ideas for Healthy Communities and Healthy Youth* (Summer 2001). See also Neil Korobov, "Ironizing Masculinity: How Adolescent Boys Negotiate Hetero-Normative Dilemmas in Conversational Interaction," *Journal of Men's Studies* 13, no. 2 (Winter 2005): 225(22) and Randolph H. Watts Jr. and L. Diane Borders, "Boys' Perceptions of the Male Role: Understanding Gender Role Conflict in Adolescent Males," *Journal of Men's Studies* 13, no. 2 (Winter 2005): 267(14).

of God's ongoing story? In short, are churches providing faithful companions to young men like Isaac, who are engaged in the long, sometimes frightening walk of growing up?

It's a guy thing:
Doing Girlfriend Theology with boys

Given this body of literature, we revisit Girlfriend Theology, a method designed for girls and women — with two new questions in mind: Around which aspects of boys' development could churches best provide helpful intervention? What would such a guy-friendly method of religious education look like? As we toyed with this question in classrooms and workshops, inviting the reflection of boys, men, and the women and girls who love them, three tentative directions for positive intervention emerged. An adapted form of Girlfriend Theology — renamed the more gender-neutral Friend Theology — seems to provide one promising way of creating such specifically "boy friendly" spaces.

Churches are particularly well suited to address one aspect of the boy code, namely, an insufficient emotional repertoire. Caring adults in small circles of storytelling and holy listening can help boys and girls imagine a larger, broader, deeper, and more robust capacity for understanding and articulating emotions. This is hard work, which presupposes a cadre of caring adults who are able to momentarily suspend their socialized expectations that "boys don't do emotions." Christian theology invites us to imagine how to be together differently. Church is a place for alternative ways of being who we really are. Churches are particularly well suited for the task of building an emotional repertoire because we are not limited to the culture's curriculum as the only vision of human possibility.

A second point of intervention is in helping boys integrate their actions in the world with reflection on inner sources of strength and wisdom. These sources include interpretations of Judeo-Christian scripture and tradition or the traditions of other world religions.

A third resource churches can offer is encouraging the practice of testimony, in which the truths of our lives are told out loud to one another.[17] This last intervention aims at revealing the great diversity we exhibit as part of God's creation. Male, female, urban, rural, working class, wealthy, of Jamaican, Filipino, or Ukrainian descent — we all reflect portions of God's story that need to be told, heard, honored, and gleaned for meaning.

With these three directives in mind, we return to the process of Girlfriend and thus Friend Theology, similar to the method of theological reflection used to lead discussions of film in chapter 4. We offer it as one possible resource caring adults in the church might use in small groups settings with the specific needs of boys in mind. The process centers around paying careful attention to true stories from the lives of real boys, and thus begins with "harvesting" such a story.

The story can be about any event that the boy has experienced, but it is best suited to stories that are *not* about religious conversions, per se. A winning football game, the death of a pet, the loss of a friend through a move or a fight, a new friendship that comes in an unexpected way; a disagreement with a parent; a day spent with a grandparent or a day spent skateboarding with a friend — any of these would be fine stories.

The adult can "harvest" the story either through a face-to-face encounter, a phone call, or by assigning the story to be written in advance. Experience tells us that the latter is sometimes intimidating, as a written assignment may seem too much like a classroom assignment and trigger failure-anxiety for less verbal or academic youth. For this reason, we find it helpful to get a volunteer in advance who is willing to tell his story, and then follow up with a phone call reminder before the actual session. We will sometimes ask the boy to tell the story to us over the phone while we type it into our computer. It is very important that the story be put down in writing for the session. This way, the story has a beginning, middle and end. Welcoming and

---

17. See Dorothy Bass and Don Richter, eds., *Way to Live: Christian Practices for Teens* (Nashville: Upper Room Books, 2002) for a discussion of the practice of testimony in the lives of youth.

modeling a relaxed and conversational tone in the group often makes it easier for boys to enter this process.

Step One: Hearing the story

In a small group of other boys and a few adults, one of whom is the designated facilitator, a boy reads his story. The participants listen carefully, noticing the ways the story reminds them of stories from their own lives. Boys are asked to pay attention to the feelings, emotions, and images that the story evokes. In Girlfriend Theology, the group gathers around a table in which a simple altar has been set and a candle has been lit to welcome God's presence. Boys might also feel drawn to gather in such a way. However, guy-friendly space might look radically different. It might be on a corner of the basketball court after engaging in a game of pick-up. It might be a scenic spot at the summit of a mountain after a rigorous hike. In our work with girls, too, an active encounter that centers us in our bodies is often a fruitful substitute for a more traditional "holy space" implied by a circle of people gathered around a candle. For instance, a group of girls who practice this method monthly in their neighborhood usually start the session with a time of vigorous jumping on one girl's trampoline.

Step Two: Feeling and naming our connections to the story

In this part of the process, we ask the boys to express the ways the story connected with them. Did they feel angry, sad, gleeful, lonely, confused? Were there places in the story where they felt reminded of a story from their own life? Did they identify strongly with one character or another? Did they laugh, cry, or feel their body grow tense? In working with girls, this step usually moves rapidly, with talking, giggling, and interruptions all intersecting. With boys, the leader might be prepared for all of the above, but also for lapses of silence and periods of goofiness. All these responses are fine, as long as we linger here long enough for the full range of emotions in the story to surface. As in other steps of the method, the adult leaders may at times need to prompt the boys if conversation is sparse.

Step Three: Looking to God, tradition, scripture, and other stories

Is there a place in the story that reminds you of God, Jesus, the Holy Spirit or some other religious imagery? Where is God in this story? What is the meaning of this story? With younger boys, this portion of the method will probably be brief. They may not have a lot of Bible stories in their memory banks — or they may not yet be capable of making the cognitive leap from lived experience to larger stories of faith and culture. That's fine. See what surfaces and then move on. This is a step that can also be open to imagery that is not explicitly religious. We often find boys wanting to relate the story to a favorite scene in a movie, such as one of the *Star Wars* adventures or one of the *Lord of the Rings* movies. Welcome this movement as "practicing" theological and thematic thinking, setting the stage for more specifically Christian theological work at a later time.

Step Four: Asking "so what?"

What does this story tell us about how we should (or should not) live our lives? What about this story might provide a guide for our future action, with our friends, family, communities, or world? How might our actions in the world be changed, redirected, or tweaked as a result of having entertained one person's story in light of God's story?

Everyone does not need to agree: differing learnings can be freed to stand beside one another. The facilitator should thoughtfully respond to each "aha moment" that is offered, prompting as many as are willing to contribute to this last step. A fruitful moment in this step is when language about call and vocation arise. Action in the world — whether that be deciding to befriend an outsider, rake leaves for an elder, or pay closer attention to issues of global warming — can all be seen as part of our vocations. The more we practice this language, the more natural it becomes. As one college student, who happens to be a pastor's kid, said in a written assignment about vocation: "This kind of talk comes easily to me. In my home, we talk about vocation every night around the dinner table."

In the steps just described, several significant changes to Girlfriend Theology have been as a result of testing the method with boys and men. This includes a more active role of the adult in "harvesting" the story. We have found that offering to "record" a story disarms boys (and girls) who might be shy about the process of writing. This step aims at welcoming and inviting participation. The adult should attempt to render the story as carefully as possible to mirror the boys' actual words. With girls, stories typically can run a page or more. But this is not necessary. Although we might aim for a page, a story may only be a couple of paragraphs. It's enough to get the process started. In one session, a junior high boy wrote a very brief story about "sk8–ing" with a friend in the fellowship hall of his church. This story led to sharing stories about trespassing — moments of doing something wrong with a friend and getting caught. They boys discussed the emotions of fear, humor, and relief surrounding such incidents in their own lives. A robust conversation about the meaning of friendship, particularly "church friends" with whom we might share experiences of unique commonality, ensued during Step Three.

Step One has been modified to allow for activity and movement. Although it is not always the case, boys sometimes respond better to activity and movement as an invitation to introspection. As one adult reported who led this step with boys during a lock-in: "They needed to first blow off steam, to do something active and noisy, before settling into a more contemplative mode." Men who work closely with young males say that engaging guys first, not just in activity, but in healthy competition, matters. Men are socialized to relate to one another through competition. Competition, while it can become excessive, can also, in the experience of some men, produce an intense form of connection that may free guys up to relax into sharing more easily.[18] When balanced with other avenues of exploring emotional terrain, competition may prove important for both males and females.

18. Thanks to students in Dori's course *Theory and Practice of Youth Ministry* at Union–PSCE for reading this chapter and engaging in a lively conversation about the unique blessings and challenges of pastoring guys.

When practicing this method with boys, Step Two is where we spend most of our time. Often in reflecting with adults about the relative success of a Friend Theology session, we will hear remarks that, if nothing else happens in the entire session, we can give thanks for the naming of feelings. Experiencing emotional talk as welcomed, respected, and celebrated may be rare in the life of any young person. It is therefore a significant contribution. Here, too, it is perfectly fine for this time to take a silly turn, a serious turn, or a silent turn. Facilitators are invited to relax and be comfortable in whatever is given and received. Emotional talk may be difficult at first, but usually becomes easier the better we get to know the boys and the more comfortable they are with each other. While it may seem intimidating to ask boys about their feelings, we find again and again that overcoming that intimidation is an important step in creating alternatives to the "boy code." Although boys may be socialized to think they don't have feelings to share, they do indeed have them. Again and again, we find guys quite willing to share those feelings, as long as a trusted adult creates an environment in which those feelings are welcomed, teased out, honored, and respected.

Step Three is often challenging for groups of people who are not naturally talkative, who may not feel well-versed in scripture, or who do not know each other well. Here, too, the more a group works together, the easier it becomes. As facilitators, we usually provide scriptures that seem to connect, if none arise from the boys themselves. When bringing up potential scriptural connections, we try to avoid being didactic. An approach that leans more toward "This connects for me; what do you think?" is helpful. A particularly meaningful conversation can occur simply around images of God that arose for boys. Perhaps there are ways in which viewing feminine or maternal imagery for God can be freeing for boys. Alternatively, boys who may have a dearth of positive male images in their lives might find great solace in perceiving God as father in new ways. It can be helpful to have a concordance and Bible on hand for those moments when someone says "It reminds me of that story from the Bible. What is it?"

This introduction to Friend Theology is brief and tentative, but allows us to begin thinking about one possible method of constructing educational spaces that take seriously boys' lives as places where God is at work. It welcomes boys to testify, telling the diverse truths of their lives out loud to one another. This is an act that, in itself, begins to break down some of the domination implied by the boy code. It allows adults to teach and model a wide emotional repertoire, addressing a key issue that boy-advocates find missing in much of boys' development. It also allows space for integrating inner wisdom with action in the world. This last step — the "aha moment" that feeds ongoing reflective action in the world — is a connection to the vital work of vocation. It is through integrating the spiritual with the lived out that we find ways to create lives of meaning and purpose.

Last summer, I (Dori) volunteered to co-lead "Friend Theology" at a day camp sponsored by an African American church in my community. One day a week, a friend and I went to the camp to meet with a group of five high school boys and girls. The first few weeks, we taught the method using clips from animated films such as *Finding Nemo, Ice Age,* and *The Incredibles.* We got to know the kids, and grew to look forward to our Thursday sessions.

After warming them to the method, we began "harvesting" stories, sitting down with one student at a time and typing his or her story onto a laptop as it was told. The young person would then quickly help edit the text, and we would bring that story for the following week's session. The girls in this group — some of whom were better able to express their emotions than the boys — seemed to almost guide the boys in teasing out emotional talk. The boys in this group — who were keenly versed in scripture — made some amazing connections between the stories and imagery of both the Hebrew Bible and the New Testament and the stories their friends told.

One particular story stands out. A thirteen-year-old boy, whom we'll call Toby, told about going to the funeral of a great-uncle who had been a prominent urban leader in Washington, D.C. Toby had never visited the city before and described the street where his uncle had lived as looking like a royal place. He went on to describe a meal at a restaurant, where the extended family lingered around the table, telling stories about the deceased uncle and enjoying one another's company.

During the emotion-sharing portion of the session, Toby expressed sadness that he had not known his great-uncle better. As the group reflected on the story, they drew on imagery of heaven as a royal city, a place where the table is groaning and family lingers in the welcoming space of one another's presence.

In this setting of both boys and girls, we glimpsed a sphere of religious education and a possibility for youth ministry. In this space, the complexities and gifts of both male and female visions of the world and of spirituality were freed to mix and mingle, breathe and dance, be carefully attended to and fully appreciated by a caring circle of young people and the adults who, briefly, for one summer, accompanied them.

The fertile soil of boy's souls: Imagining other guy-friendly spaces

Several years ago, faced with a mostly male Sunday school classroom full of wiggly, active, restless ten- and eleven-year-old boys, I ditched the printed curriculum and dragged the kids outside to a sunny spot of grass. There we planted a garden where we could meet and revisit the parable of the sower (Matt. 13:1–9). In one corner of the garden was a bramble of thorns, where the seeds we dropped were choked. Another spot was full of rocks, a place where sprouts would get scorched by the sun. Through the middle was a path of round garden stones, where we sprinkled seeds for the birds to eat. In the center of the garden was thick, orange Virginia clay — our own little patch of fertile soil.

The garden was indeed fertile soil for three seasons of Sunday school as we tilled, planted, weeded, watered, nurtured, and harvested tomatoes, zucchini, and mammoth sunflowers. After enjoying what we came to call our Fertile Soil garden, the kids persuaded me

to plant again the next year. We enlisted the little children during
midwinter, asking them to bury our seeds in clear plastic Dixie cups
filled with dirt. This time, we called it the Taste and See (Ps. 34:8)
garden. We looked at scripture in the Hebrew Bible, particularly the
psalms and the prophets that point to the earth as a source of wisdom
and abundant fruitfulness. We shared our harvest with the congregation by making a big pot of Stone Soup, acting out the popular folk
tale and then enjoying a simple meal together.

There was a particular tomato plant in our Sunday school garden
the last year we planted. We came to call it our Good Samaritan plant.
We found it one day in June, sprouting up where it didn't belong. It
was a volunteer, growing from the seed of last year's tomato, fallen
and left to rot on the ground. To Win, who had pointed it out, I
suggested that he might want to pull it up, freeing up the space so
its neighbor could flourish. But Win, our most experienced gardener,
decided instead to gently transplant it to a place where it would have
room to grow. I shrugged my shoulders, accustomed by now to my
having my gardening advice justifiably questioned or ignored.

Later that same day, while our hands were busy weeding, Win
told us about an experience he had had the day before. During an
annual outdoor festival at a nearby park, Win had been standing
with his mother in line to buy a funnel cake when they both noticed
that the woman making the funnel cakes was becoming overcome
with heat. A few minutes later, she collapsed. With a nod from his
mother, Win ran off to find emergency personnel, who briefly treated
the woman and carried her away in a golf cart. It was a frightening
experience, but Win knew he had been in the right place at the right
time. During our closing prayer circle that day, Win prayed for the
unknown woman, and we thanked God that Win had been chosen
as an agent of God's healing in the midst of a crowded, sweaty mass
of people waiting to buy funnel cake

Over a month later, as we battled weeds that had overtaken our
garden during weeks of neglect, I spotted Win's transplanted volunteer. It was laden with heavy green fruit. We all gathered around
it, amazed that a plant almost plucked up as an intruder had been

transformed through Win's attention and now promised a great harvest.

Win's vocation as a helper and a good gardener emerged in part because we moved out of our heads and into our bodies during a season of Sundays. Boys, who in U.S. society are at high risk of being diagnosed with a host of behavioral disorders, bring a particular set of needs to the spaces where we shape and form Christian beliefs and practices. This story of Win and his classmates, immersed in a project involving body, mind, and soul, stands as a metaphor for hopeful ways in which educational spaces might change in order to make space for the particular needs of boys as their vocations emerge in a day and time when they are less likely than girls to go to college, and in which the working-class jobs that were once available to high school graduates no longer exist. The garden project was literally and figuratively indigenous to the little church, made up of mostly white, middle-class folks, where I belong. What other projects — aimed at better reaching young men in other communities — are springing up elsewhere?

Walking with Isaac

Jay's reflection on Isaac's long walk with his dad directs attention to a troublesome text, one that the sensitive preacher, teacher, and exegete in all of us is tempted to avoid. What kind of God would pull such a prank, taking a loving father to the brink of murder, just to test his loyalty? Or, as Win's Sunday school class asked upon hearing this story as if for the first time, "Why in the world would a loving God require this test? Why in the world would God even pretend that Abraham was supposed to kill Isaac? Why did God let it go so far — even to the point of tying Isaac up — before revealing the hidden plan of sacrificing a ram instead? *Why* in the world is this story in the Bible, which is supposed to be about *love?*"[19] These are all good

---

19. As this story approached for a class engaged in a slow reading of the Book of Genesis, the season of Advent also drew near. I (Dori) told the children there

questions, given the history of interpretations in which this text has been understood to equate a father's faithfulness with his willingness to sacrifice his son.

Scripture never means only one thing. It was only upon living with this text long enough to find a satisfying answer for children — who must hear loudly and clearly in church classrooms that God *never* wants grown-ups to harm them — that a truth to hold on to emerged. In this alternative reading of the Genesis account — the oldest form of a story that appears three more times in Exodus — we see Yahweh defining a new kind of deity. This deity, over against the plethora of deities worshiped in surrounding cults, decidedly rejects this ultimate sacrifice. *This* deity doesn't see a human life as expendable, but as ultimately significant, indeed the key to covenantal promise-keeping. Clearly, this God isn't like all the other deities in the neighborhood.

Thank God for the ram in the thicket, the children said. And, above all, thank God that Abraham was open to a new way of thinking, a new way for the story to end. He was flexible enough to change plans — to withdraw the knife already in hand — when he heard the voice of an angel. Perhaps God wanted this story in the Bible to show precisely how different Yahweh was and is from all the other gods on the market. Perhaps, even today, there are other gods being worshiped in our neighborhoods, cities, and suburban malls. Perhaps we sometimes come dangerously close to sacrificing the most important things in life — time with family, devotion to friends and loved ones, passionate engagement with our neighbors in need and an earth in need of mending — for the gods of wealth, status, consumption, greed, nationalism, and desire. Isaac's story is one that calls us to wake up to what we do or almost do to the ones we love when we follow, unquestioningly, a script that seems predetermined.

This Genesis God who still reveals God's self in the lives of young ones coming to vocational expression today does not require that we sacrifice our young. This God, instead, made a huge sacrifice that

---

was an important, frightening story coming up in our Bible, one requiring parental guidance. This stirred a lot of interest. We lapsed into Advent teaching, returning to Abraham and Isaac with the new year and, significantly, a savior born.

resounds throughout the corridors of history. In giving us a savior — one who lived out his calling fully in all that he did — God reminds us that we, too, have a calling. As one college senior reflecting on his call wrote: "Our vocation is how we allow God and God's message to work through us in a similar manner to how Jesus was the ultimate manifestation of God's message to humanity."

We see convincing evidence that boys need, want, and create intimacy in their lives. They are seeking ways to be masculine that do not prevent them from engaging in care-taking, give-and-take relationship, and life-giving solidarity in the midst of cultural and societal forces that threaten to place them in the "gender straitjacket." The church can be a place that embraces boys as they are — with all the diversity they exhibit. It can also be place that challenges and changes the definition of "boy."

Given its distinctively theological framing of life's meaning and purpose, the church is capable of guiding boys in the difficult work of constructing their identity, especially when that results in vocational choices or directions that write a new story. Jay as a Christian educator and Toby as a kid who wishes to know better the extended family provide important reminders to those of us who hope to companion youth. Boys' stories of intimacy, attentiveness, and wonder lie in wait for moments that welcome self-disclosure. Boys long to see their stories as part of God's unfolding story. It is our task — like it was Abraham's — to stay open to messengers that would stay our hands mid-sacrifice, directing us away from the violence and destruction that often claims men's lives. The redirection leads us on a long walk home, in which we find companions to help us on our way.

We have looked at the way young people — male and female — long to see their story as part of God's unfolding story. Our final chapter further explores this concept of vocation within Christian theology. How do young people reshape the notion of call, rewrite Christian tradition, interact with saints and sages, as they live out vocations calling for this new day?

Chapter 8

Whose calling? Who's calling?

The Spirit of God and the calling of youth

My fourth-grader recently brought home an assignment. He needed
to make a list of words used around our house that are contrac-
tions — words such as "it's," "don't," or "can't" that combine two
words into one. And so that afternoon, when he heard me (Joyce)
answer the telephone and ask, "Who is calling, please?" Micah ea-
gerly brought over his homework paper with a question: "If we made
a contraction out of 'who is,' would it be *'who's calling'* or *'whose
calling'*? They sound the same."

Later that evening, after Micah and his two siblings were fast
asleep, I sat with my cup of hot tea and piles of books, reflecting
on the central theological theme of this book, vocation. As I read a
passage from Paul's letter to the church at Corinth concerning gifts
given by the Spirit of God to be used for the common good (1 Cor.
12), Micah's question came back to me full force. There are, in fact,
always *two* questions Christians must address when we talk about
the call to use our lives and gifts in the service of God: Who's calling? Whose calling? These questions literally do sound the same. They
also "sound the same" in the metaphorical sense of being inextricably
bound up with each other: it is impossible to talk meaningfully about
vocation and youth in the church without addressing together these
connected questions about the Caller and the called. We can never
fully consider one of them without at the same time accounting for
the other.

The first question, "Who's calling?" asks about the One who issues
the call to live faithful lives of hope, joy, and holy struggle. It is the

side of vocation concerned with the identity and work of God who gives us gifts to use for the common good, and then places a claim on us to do so. Asking "who's calling?" leads us to wonder not only *what* are the purposes of God in which human beings may participate, but also *how* does God work today to stir youth and adults to offer their lives for the flourishing of the whole creation.

The second question, "Whose calling?" asks about the identity of the ones who hear and respond to God's claim. When asked in relation to youth in the church, "whose calling?" also emphasizes whether (and how) the call to vocation comes to people of all ages, even and especially to the young.

Throughout this book, we attend carefully to the voices and stories of young people seeking to walk in God's way. We have gently eavesdropped as young women and men described their yearnings toward meaningful ways to offer their gifts and their lives in service, care, justice, and compassion. Out of these stories of graced struggle by youth, we find fresh insights concerning a Christian theology of vocation. This constitutes a significant contribution that young people make to such a theology. Listening closely to them has renewed our awareness that young people are indispensable to ongoing efforts to shape and reshape Christian theology and its accompanying practices.

Adolescence, a time within the human lifespan when persons appear particularly open to religious experience and encounters with God in the here and now, has the potential to be a *kairos*-time in human life. That is, it can be a period of life ripe with the sense of God's presence and calling, a time of deep sensitivity and openness to the purposes and activity of God.

It makes sense, therefore, that young people have some particular contributions to make to the wider church's theological understandings of Christian vocation. In this final chapter, then, we lift up three insights gleaned from young people and the experiences they share with us, as youthful contributions to a contemporary Christian theology of vocation:

1. Vocation is first and foremost about using God-given gifts in every aspect of one's life for the flourishing of the whole creation. It therefore refers to a journey and an identity. It can never be reduced to career or work alone.

2. Vocation is communal. Even though persons may experience and respond to God's call as individuals, Christian vocation is never a solitary enterprise.

3. God calls youth *as the young people they are* — i.e., Christian youth have life-purposes that exist within the purposes of God not in spite of their young age, but because of it. The vocation of youth in the church and in the world places young people in a distinctively prophetic role that is necessary to the life and transformation of both the church and the world.

Gifts, not work...at least not only *work*

In contemporary speech, the term "vocation" has come to be closely associated with work, career, and profession. Stripped of its theological meanings, vocation often operates like a synonym for work in its secular usages. Vocational schools prepare people to take on certain types of work. Vocational counseling helps individuals sort out their job interests and preferences, toward choosing the best career path. And in the United States, where sociologists note that people are extraordinarily obsessed with work and give it undue importance in determining their sense of worth and identity, there exists a strong pull to understand vocation in terms of work. Even among Christians for whom the term "vocation" possesses a distinctly religious connotation, there is still a primary sense in which the issue of one's calling concerns making sure one does the right kind of work.

Of course, theologians hold some of the blame for this conflation between work and vocation. Martin Luther retrieved the notion of vocation from its narrow uses in the medieval church to describe the callings of persons to religious orders and the priesthood, claiming that all types of labor and all stations in life could be holy callings.

Likewise, John Calvin affirmed the "priesthood of all believers" and with it the idea that God calls men and women to Christian service through many kinds of work, not just through ordained office in the church. In both instances, these reformers were attempting to create a contrast between the idea that only some Christians have vocations (i.e., priests, nuns, and monks), and the idea that God calls all Christians in their baptisms. Making their case by contrasting ordained office with other forms of work, however, created a legacy in which the association between vocation and paid labor remains strong.

Sociologists deem the United States a society obsessed with work, in which people find their primary identities through the work they do. "What do you do?" is one of the first questions asked of strangers on airplanes and at parties. Americans spend more time working than virtually any other activity even when the need to earn a livelihood is not the reason for working harder or longer. Into such a cultural context, the Protestant theological propensity to consecrate work by calling it vocation seems right at home. Problematically, this leads to a situation in which we in the church forget that while work may be one important site where persons live out their vocations, the work itself is not the vocation.

In recent times, the perspective associating the call of God so exclusively with work has been widely critiqued by many feminist and third world theologians as elitist or as potentially sanctifying the unjust structuring of labor. The danger that such a notion of vocation can be used to create a religious justification for encouraging people to accept dehumanizing or oppressive forms of work as God's calling is significant. Using the concept of vocation to "baptize" social divisions between groups (e.g., the idea that certain classes of people fulfill their divine calling by performing menial work) is far from the view of God's call for people to use their gifts we see as so central to Christian faith.

But there remains still another reason the pull to understand vocation exclusively or primarily in terms of work appears problematic. While many young people do participate in the paid labor force, adult work, career, and profession for the most part remain future-tense events for them. Associating vocation with adult labor means, for the most part, *dis*associating youth from vocation. It renders adolescence merely preparatory.

Of course there *is* a strong future orientation to the Christian idea of vocation: to be called is to be drawn toward something different from where and how one already lives. Paul and other New Testament letter writers speak of "the hope to which God has called you" (Eph. 1:18), or name the believers "you who are called to be saints" (1 Cor. 1:2; Rom. 1:7). Vocation has a future face as it directs the lives of believers toward the fulfillment of God's desires for the creation, a fulfillment that is not known or experienced fully now, and which therefore is still future. Vocation bears an eschatological fingerprint.

The future-related aspect of vocation, however, in no way excludes youth from being called by God. Churches whose primary orientation toward youth is to see them as a pool of "future members or leaders" fail to grasp the present and immediate quality that operates within and alongside the future element in Christian understandings of vocation. The idea of "being called" by God sometimes appears in Paul's writings as a shorthand way to refer to a person's initial encounter with the invitation to walk in the way of Jesus, as Paul puts it, "when you were called" or "at the time you were called" (1 Cor. 7).

In that sense, vocation as the "call from God" is something that every Christian receives through baptism. In that ritual we "put on a new identity in Christ," one that has present-day consequences in the life of the believer. Adults, children, and youth receive this new identity in Christ through their calling. Paul's linguistic way of conveying this link between the call and identity is to use the term *klesis*, or call as a *name*: he refers to the Christians in Corinth as *oi kletoi*, those who are called. Being called becomes their name, their identity. In fact, the very term used for church in the New Testament, *ecclesia*, literally means "the called-out ones." God gives us gifts that equip us to live out that one call in lots of different and particular ways. So we read the writer of Ephesians saying, "The gifts he gave were that some would be apostles, some prophets, some evangelists, some pastors and teachers, to equip the saints for the work of ministry" (Eph. 4:11). Those particularities are certainly part of the call, but they derive from the one call of God to new life in Christ.

As Karl Barth starkly put it, vocation is the signature distinguishing the Christian from the non-Christian: "the goal of vocation is not a special Christian existence, but the existence of the Christian as such, and that the existence of the Christian is either grounded in his vocation or not at all."[1] The specific ways our lives are marked by God's grace — i.e., the relationships we have, the kinds of work we do, like youth ministry or nursing or carpentry, the patterns of living and stewardship that make up our way of witnessing to the world — all these come from the particular gifts God's Spirit bestows and from the continuing renewal of our call, such that our identity in Christ really is "new every morning." Although our salvation rests in God alone, our response to that salvation is always lived out in actions and practices, ways of being and behaving, that mark us as the body of Christ alive for today.

In his letter to the Romans, Paul asserts that God's call is "according to God's purpose" (8:28). He then goes on, in a passage simultaneously responsible for both the theological brilliance and major theological conundrum within the Reformed tradition of Christian faith, to claim that people called by God are not only "chosen" but "predestined" to participate in God's larger providential purposes on a cosmic scale: "We know that all things work together for good for those who love God, who are called according to God's purpose. For those whom God foreknew, God also predestined to be conformed to the image of the Son, in order that he might be the firstborn within a large family [literally 'many brothers']. And those whom God predestined, God also called; and those whom God called, God also justified; and those whom God justified, God also glorified."

---

1. Karl Barth, *Church Dogmatics*, trans. A. T. Mackay, T. H. L. Parker, Harold Knight, Henry A. Kennedy, and John Marks (Edinburgh: T. & T. Clark, 1961), 4:3.ii, 524.

This Pauline notion of vocation seems to work against the idea that our vocations are much of our own making. Paul foregrounds the question, "Who's calling?" For Paul, it is God who does the calling; God into whose purposes our human volition is enfolded; God whose purposes are cosmic in scope and far beyond our grasp. The bottom line for Paul is that God is the one who calls us, and our call comes out of God's choosing us.

Walter Brueggemann once remarked that sooner or later all questions of identity become questions of vocation.[2] The question of who we are eventually becomes a question about human purpose, a question of *whose* we are; a question of why it should even matter *that* we are. Most of us are well aware of adolescence as a time of identity formation, to use Erik Erikson's terminology. If Brueggemann is right, then it should not surprise us to learn that adolescence is also a time of intense religious interest and searching: questions of who one is and whose one is together take on heightened significance. The double questions of who's calling and whose calling do indeed sound the same when it comes to youth. Unfortunately, though, instead of seeing the teen years as *kairos* time, when the developmentally shaped quest for identity and a sense of purpose collides with God's call, churches inadvertently put youth into an extended "time out."

Far too often, instead of inviting youth into the companioned walk we call vocation, youth ministry has sent them on a vacation — an extended trip with the primary goals of keeping youth occupied, entertained, and distracted — until such time as they become adults.

While many of the young men and women whose stories shape the pages of this book do indeed focus attention on the (future) kinds of work for which they are preparing, without exception these youth also understand themselves to be living out their vocations to serve God in their everyday lives here and now. Holly in her quest for a college that embodies an ethic of care for the land, Garrett in his avid seeking of common ground across the spectrum of evangelical and liberal churches, and Cara in desiring to be like her Latin

---

2. Ibid., 125.

American grandmother, who constantly gives away her scant material possessions — these stories and others point to the simultaneously *already*-and-not-yet aspects of vocation.

These young persons are not waiting until adulthood or until they land a "real job" to make sense of what they do and how they live in terms of God's calling of them. Rather, they speak and act in terms of a present-tense discernment of God's call, a call that cuts across every area of life, not just work.

What these young people invite the church to remember about vocation, then, is that responding to God's call is not the same thing as participating in the paid labor force as an adult. Instead, vocation concerns participation in the life of God, across the whole spectrum of human experience. These youth give witness to the New Testament understanding of calling as the recognition of gifts coupled with the mandate to use those gifts on behalf of the world that God created, broods over, and loves. One hopes that these youth and their adult companions *will* find ways that their paid work might be a site for using God's gifts in service — just as they find ways to offer their gifts in their relationships, in play and leisure, in situations of struggle and conflict, in care for the earth and compassion for the "least and last" of society.

God's call: To Individuals, through communities

Lois Lowry's novel *The Giver*, describes a future society in which children at each age are recognized in an annual ceremony for the new abilities emerging at that age level.[3] Around age nine, the community elders begin to observe the children carefully as they go about their schooling, play, and expected volunteer service, in order to discern their gifts. At the "ceremony of twelves," the elders identify the kind of life-work chosen for that young person, based on a match between the youngster's gifts and the needs of the community. Certainly in Lowry's novel there is a distopian side to this communal process of

---

3. Louis Lowry, *The Giver* (Boston: Houghton Mifflin, 1993).

calling young people into service. The main character, Jonas, finds himself thrust into a role that requires him to bear the communal memory of the group, including all its pain, in ways that are extremely detrimental to him as an individual.

At the same time, however, Lowry's image of communal discernment of gifts remains evocative of how persons are called. Time and time again, the youth whose stories populate these pages remind us that multiple others — parents, teachers, aunts and uncles, youth ministers, coaches, friends — help them to imagine, know, claim, and use their gifts. As Douglas Schuurman puts it, God calls people through various "mediators."[4] Instead of coming to persons as a "miraculous, unmistakable word of direction," God's call most often comes "mediated by nature, family, community, friends."[5]

James Fowler has suggested that "our most serious modern heresy [is] the individualistic assumption that we are or can be *self-grounded persons*. This assumption means believing that we have within us — and are totally responsible for generating from within us — all the resources out of which to create a fulfilled and self-actualized life."[6]

What Fowler rightly addresses here is the tendency for persons to believe that we "write our own lives." This is the myth of the great American self-made person. We are formed by the idea that we simply make up our minds and act; that humans shape their own destinies and are fully agents of their own lives without constraints. This idea came as refreshing news to us as young women who looked at our mothers' generation and wished for more self-authorship. However, we sometimes act as if we write our lives alone, as if we have no constraints. In fact, all of our lives are shaped by concrete circumstances that pose both possibility and limit. And some people, by virtue of where they were born and to whom, have more limits than

---

4. Douglas J. Schuurman, *Vocation: Discerning Our Callings in Life* (Grand Rapids, Mich.: William B. Eerdmans, 2004), 37.

5. Ibid., 127.

6. James Fowler, *Becoming Adult, Becoming Christian: Adult Development and Christian Faith* (San Francisco: Harper & Row, 1984), 101–2.

others. Some people inherit white privilege while others must nego-tiate racist barriers to their thriving. All of this unmasks the lie of self-actualization.

Christians claim a corrective: in our call *God* rewrites our lives; that we have new lives formed and reformed as the story of Christ begins to take shape in us. Paul writes about vocation as the work of the Holy Spirit (1 Cor. 12). As such, it is not something youth or adults "achieve." Nor is it static, a matter of "been there, done that." Vocation is something that God's Spirit directs and redirects in persons. As Fowler puts it, "Vocation, seen as a call to partnership with God on behalf of the neighbor, constitutes a far more fruitful way to look at the question of our specialness, our giftedness, and our possibilities of excellence."[7] In other words, in our vocations it is not only *we* who act, but also God who acts in us — making it possible for our lives to join God's outpouring of love-in-action for the world.

That is a rather countercultural perspective to North American so-cial norms that proclaim a meritocracy, a pervasive myth that our successes are earned. In a meritocracy we supposedly achieve things because we merit them. Persons seem to take charge of their own destinies in purposeful ways. The white male who quickly climbs the corporate ladder need never acknowledge the inheritance of privilege that gave him a head start. It may be the case that a fair amount of the low self-esteem and depression experienced by so many youth — especially girls and youth of color in the United States — comes from the stark recognition that they themselves do not possess all the nec-essary resources to construct a meaningful and fulfilling life. Nor does the culture offer them such resources.

For these and other youth, the Christian meaning of vocation, of being called, offers hope. Hope resides in the belief that identity and worth come from who we are in God — "the called ones" — and not in the narrow, circumscribed identities offered by the world.

---

7. Ibid., 102.

Womanist practical theologian Evelyn Parker uses the term "eman-cipatory hope" to describe this already but not yet inbreaking of God's new creation.[8] Parker takes seriously the suffering that black youth experience. In the midst of this very suffering she offers a vision of Christian faith that avoids pie-in-the-sky wishful thinking. When black youth come to see themselves as participants in the Christian story, they glimpse the capacity to live into the creative justice of God. This means learning to confront racist structures, subvert dominant norms, and envision themselves as agents of change in the here and now, while also anticipating the expected future of God.

The particular calling of youth

Above, we identified two contributions young people make to a Christian theology of vocation. The first of these involves an under-standing of divine calling as encompassing our God-given gifts. These are shared with the world in all of what we do, not through ca-reer or job alone. The second contribution draws greater attention to the communal shape of vocation, and the critical role of "medi-ators" through whom God's Spirit works to call Christians to lives of faith. The final contribution concerns our understanding that God calls and uses persons at all ages of life, working with the particu-lar *charisms* of that age, to accomplish God's work on behalf of the whole creation. If we take this last contribution seriously, we sharpen our understanding of eschatology in significant ways.

With constructive developmental thinkers such as Robert Kegan, even as we criticize rigidly defined designations of age groups as masked social constructions, we nevertheless may note the integrity and genius of particular ages. The characterization of youth as in-herently rebellious, troubled, and troubling has come under scrutiny, thankfully. At the same time, however, there remains some sense in which the probing questions, openness to new possibilities, energy,

---

8. Evelyn Parker, *Trouble Don't Last Always: Emancipatory Hope among African American Adolescents* (Cleveland: Pilgrim Press), 2003.

and fearlessness associated with young people constitutes a charism — a distinct gift — of adolescence.

Certainly the twentieth-century theologian Karl Barth saw adolescence as having its own charism, which was much-needed by both church and world. We offer his words from the *Church Dogmatics,* in spite of the exclusively male-gendered language in which Barth wrote them, as an important example of a systematic theologian's attention to the religious vocations of young women and men:

> To the concept of the vocation in which the calling of God already finds man there belongs the clear and definite element of his age.... That the young man is still relatively without experience means that he is not in such danger of already being the slave of habit, chained to a routine and therefore traditionalistic, sophisticated, relativistic or skeptical. He should be capable of a certain independence, of a fruitful astonishment, of a measure of faith.... He should not be the victim of boredom because everything is so familiar. The thought of impotence in the face of a blind fate should be far from him. He is also lacking in materials to make a picture of himself, to think out his particular role and to learn it off — notions which he might be tempted to make normative for his future...Will he see and grasp his opportunity?[9]

In Barth's estimation, the *age* of youth, that is, the very youthfulness of youth, offers a unique opportunity for Christian vocation. The truth of this claim appears to be borne out in the examples of young people we interviewed and worked with in congregations. Two stories come to mind.

Daniel, age eleven, raised a flock of chickens in his backyard during the four years he was a member of Dori's Sunday school and

---

9. Karl Barth, *Church Dogmatics,* trans. A. T. Mackay, T. H. L. Parker, Harold Knight, Henry A. Kennedy, and John Marks (Edinburgh: T. & T. Clark, 1961), 3:4, 607, 612. The male-gendered pronouns of the original translation are preserved in this quotation. However, we would apply Barth's discussion of youthful vocation to both girls and boys.

confirmation classes. She fondly remember his glee a few years back as the class harvested giant sunflowers from a garden, planted by the children to experience Jesus' parable of the sower (Matt. 13). "Can I take some of these home and feed them to my chickens?" Daniel asked with anticipation. The class members decided this would be a fine use of the garden's bounty. A few months later, during a conversation about vocation, Daniel expressed his desire to be a farmer when he grows up. Shortly afterward, he began bringing his free-range eggs to church. In exchange for $1.50, congregation members can enjoy serving Daniel's eggs in their weekend omelets.

Daniel may indeed become a full-time farmer some day. Or he may be a teacher or a doctor who raises flocks of chickens in his spare time. In between now and then, he is about the work God calls him to do. Beyond studying for a science test and making his bed each morning, Daniel feeds, waters, and cares for his chickens. As he watches a mother hen gather her brood under her wings and shares stories of new life emerging in the incubator, Daniel is, like Jesus, learning from his chicken-neighbors about the very nature of God.[10]

In the moment Daniel's mind sparked the connection between a plentiful harvest of seeds and his hungry chickens, we see Barth's "fruitful astonishment" in action. Vocation, in light of this story, bears theological imprints of the future, because it glimpses a day and time when there will be a bounteous harvest, with plenty of food for all. But it also stands complete in the present as one young person's delight bears gifts he offers back to his world.

Dori's daughter, Erin, ten, was aghast a few winters ago over reports about the plight of monarch butterflies, whose migratory patterns have been affected by deforestation, biochemically engineered farming, and overdevelopment of formerly natural habitats. She spent hours emailing experts across the country to learn what she could do to help. In addition to encouraging others to plant flower gardens

---

10. For a beautiful essay description of the capacity of winged creatures to teach us about the Holy One, see Barbara Brown Taylor, "Barnyard Behavior," *Christian Century*, September 19, 2006, 35.

that attract and feed monarchs, she learned about the importance of planting native milkweed that hosts the monarch chrysalis. That Advent, she spent hours in her kitchen with her favorite CD playing, as she molded and painted plaster butterfly ornaments for friends and family, attaching a milkweed seedpod, instructions for planting, and an emphatic "Butterflies need YOUR help" to each gift.

Instead of fruitful astonishment, we might name Erin's impulse fascinated horror. She was horrified to learn that a species might disappear in her lifetime, and she was fascinated to discover she might have a role to play in protecting it. Her concern — tinged by a certain idealism characteristic of one who hasn't yet studied the Holocaust, Watergate, or the depletion of the Amazon rainforest — unfolds as potential gift to the world.

Erin's interest in butterflies may indeed unfold in a future career as an environmental scientist, but that is almost entirely beside the point. In her responsiveness to a perceived need, she followed a voice within — a whisper or a shout — calling her to love-in-action on behalf of God's creation. In Barth's words, that takes a "measure of faith" that many adults would be too busy, preoccupied, skeptical, or jaded to embrace.

What these young people contribute to a Christian theology of vocation, then, is the affirmation that God calls youth *as the young people they are*. In this perspective, youth called by God have life-purposes that exist within the purposes of God — not in spite of their young age but because of it. The vocation of youth in the church and in the world places young people in a distinctively prophetic role that is necessary to the life and transformation of both the church and the world. If we acknowledge that *youth* have an "already" vocation, and not merely a "not yet" vocation, then we must also recognize that elderly persons and children have a calling in the here and now too.

This contribution invites us to reconsider the way we tell time. We generally use *chronos* time, the linear path that locates events in the past, present, and future. In this way of marking time the future, in which God's transformation will be accomplished, stands starkly

separate from the present. For Christians, however, the Pauline understanding of "realized eschatology" urges us to tell time differently.
Paul imagines God's transformation of creation as both already
breaking into our lives in the present and as not yet fully accomplished. God's call to youth is already happening. It is not some future
only, pie-in-the-sky event to be achieved later. Neither is it fully lived
out now. When we turn adolescence into a waiting period for a vocation that will transpire only in adulthood, we work in *chronos* time.
A *kairos* understanding of the vocations of youth asserts, instead,
that God already calls Daniel and Erin, youth who are already living
into their gifts, although not fully.

If we take this seriously, we can envision an important corrective
to currently popular apocalyptic worldviews that hasten ecological
destruction and see wars in the Middle East as part of a divine plan.
God's hope for creation, like young people's vocations, is not "on
hold" awaiting a future moment. It is in-process, ever-evolving, available in glimpses, akin to those rare and cherished moments when we
experience perfect balance in the tensions of our vocational pursuits.
Our family, home, work and pleasure — on fleeting occasions — co-
here beautifully. They dance gracefully, confirming the mysterious
blend of choice and givens that make us who we are. Before the
next day, we may find ourselves again in the midst of struggle and
incoherence, but the touchstone moment remains.

The public shape of youthful gifts

So much has changed in the world since September 11, 2001, including how we make sense of the time of life we call adolescence.
Unfortunately, both of us authors have had to spend a fair amount of
time in airports since the terrorist attacks on the World Trade Center
and the Pentagon. One of the most striking changes in our minds from
those initial months following the attacks was that eighteen-year-olds
toting "walkmans," wearing baggy jeans with not-too-obviously-
intentional rips in the knees, and playing Frisbee down the corridors
of airports were for many months replaced by eighteen-year-olds

carrying semi-automatic weapons, wearing army camouflage, and not playing anything.

We live in a world in which Erik Erikson's concept of "moratorium" seems vastly inadequate. Treating adolescents as adults-in-training seems to delay a young person's potential to contribute — perhaps even to intervene in critical ways — on behalf of a world in need. This disempowered, non-contributing identity denies the fragility of human life, the urgency of persons offering their gifts to the world while they still have life and breath to do so.

I (Joyce) recall during my years as a mission co-worker in the Philippines watching a young man of about fifteen or sixteen standing in the rain on the streets of Manila at the edge of a large area of land populated by the urban poor of that city. This young man was drawing the runoff water from the gutter into a makeshift bucket and pouring it over his head for a shower — once, twice, but the third bucket went not over his head but up to his lips as drinking water, the only drinking water to which he had access. For this young man and millions other like him, adolescence has never been a moratorium. Perhaps it is fair to say that for him and others like him, adolescence has never really existed, has never been able to have the layers of meaning it has in middle-class, white U.S. society. The so-called sufferings of privileged adolescents in the American middle- and affluent classes quickly pale in relation to youth like this one who never experience Erikson's moratorium in any shape or form. How can we make sense of such complexities without trivializing one in light of the other?

We cannot put a good spin on the horror of September 11, falsely creating redemptive meanings out of senseless human suffering. We can, however, seek transformed visions of everyday reality that result from the forced vulnerability that day brought. For some Americans, loss and pain are ample reason to retreat into isolationism and militarism. An alternative response is solidarity with the marginalized youth of many cultures in our own nation and around the world. For so many of them, adolescence has never been a moratorium. Their everyday lives are skewed by violence.

Solidarity refers to the practice of standing with others, particularly with others unlike ourselves, identifying with them and their situation. It implies a relationship of connection amid difference. It suggests that even though we may not share in a particular condition or situation in our own lives (e.g., economic poverty, constant exposure to violence), we can choose to "stand with" those who are so affected as a witness to God's action in Christ of standing with the oppressed of the earth. American youth who felt grief, vulnerability, anger, and horror over the attacks of September 11, 2001, can empathically identify with people elsewhere in the U.S. and around the globe who daily experience such realities. Youth who served on mission trips in the aftermath of Hurricane Katrina demonstrated exactly this kind of compassion and empathy in their activist solidarity that rebuilt churches, houses, and schools in repeated trips to this devastated area of the United States. The practice of solidarity, born in empathic regard for the situations of others, leads youth to a public expression of gifts.

"Now there are varieties of gifts, but the same Spirit; and there are varieties of services, but the same Lord; and there are varieties of activities, but it is the same God who activates all of them in everyone. To each is given the manifestation of the Spirit for the common good" (1 Cor. 12:4–7). These gifts are not private possessions or individual achievements to be capitalized on with the next career move. Instead, Paul says, these gifts "activated in everyone by God" are to be used for the good of the whole community.

What this common, public character of Christian vocation suggests about the call of youth is that youth, in order to be faithful to their vocations, need to be able to offer their gifts for the common good. It seems that in every crisis, in every war, in every moment of institutional transition, young people have played a prophetic role of calling the society to look at what the society preferred not to see. There are some scholars who believe that this historic role of youth as the "voice of dissent" and the social conscience of the culture has been eroded considerably, as social, political, economic, and religious instability exert a silencing effect on young people.[11] Others believe this silence is the result of a "trivialization" of young people's aspirations — a result of a constant barrage of marketing, convincing youth that the prime goal in life is to be entertained, be that by the ever-present electronic screen or by the various sporting industries that willingly consume youth passions.[12] Regardless of the cause of the silence, many adults will grant that it is far easier and far more comfortable for adults to live without the nagging voices of youth who notice problems and dare to ask why; who see hypocrisies and dare to challenge them. When we relax into that comfortable silence, especially in the church, we do so at our own peril.

Remember Jeremiah's call?

> Now the word of the Lord came to me saying, "Before I formed you in the womb I knew you, and before you were born I consecrated you; I appointed you a prophet to the nations." Then I said, "Ah, Lord God! Truly I do not know how to speak for I am only a youth." But the Lord said to me, "Do not say, 'I am only a youth'; for you shall go to all whom I send you, and you shall speak whatever I command you. Do not be afraid of them, for I am with you to deliver you, says the Lord." (Jer. 1:4– 8)

As with the call of Jeremiah, the *prophetic vocation of youth* in the church concerns the capacities of young people to call the church back to its mission and to envision anew for every new age the shape and character of Christian witness. There are numerous examples from the youth we listen to, in which the deep hungers of youth

---

11. See Michael Warren, *Seeing through the Media: A Religious View of Communications and Cultural Analysis* (Harrisburg, Pa: Trinity Press International, 1997), and also his earlier work, *Youth, Gospel, Liberation* (New York: Veritas, 1987), especially chapter 2. Mike A. Males also addresses this issue from a secular and somewhat more polemical angle in *Framing Youth: Ten Myths about the Next Generation* (Monroe, Me.: Common Courage Press), 1999.

12. Warren, *Youth, Gospel, Liberation;* an excellent recent treatment of youth and consumer culture may be found in Katherine Turpin, *Branded: Adolescents Converting from Consumer Faith* (Cleveland: Pilgrim Press), 2006.

for God reshape the way of being the church in a particular place, as youth's prophetic role and voice, the prophetic capacity of the yearnings and desires of youth, call the church to an alternative way. Or as Letty Russell puts it, these youth "subvert the church into being the church."[13] That is the special charism and prophetic function of the call of youth.

Part of the challenge for young people concerns the way that churches resist this charism of youth, preferring instead to channel their energies into domesticated practices of church life and youth ministry that risk little and change less. Sharon Daloz Parks, writing on young people who are "twenty-something" and beyond, puts it this way:

> Too many of our young adults are not being encouraged to ask the big questions that awaken critical thought in the first place. Swept up in religious assumptions that remain unexamined (and economic assumptions that function religiously), they easily become vulnerable to the conventional cynicism of our time or to the economic and political agendas of a consumption-driven yet ambivalent age.[14]

In a culture that persuasively presents "good consumer" as a primary vocation of youth, it is all too easy for the church to simply invite young people to become good consumers of church, instead of inviting them to live out their calling. A congregation practicing as "an ecology of vocations," to use Fowler's term, would be a place where youth and adults together ask big questions and dream worthy dreams; where the community can bless the call of youth, make room for the prophetic witness of youth, and accompany young people on their ever unfolding vocational journeys.

---

13. See Letty M. Russell, *Church in the Round: Feminist Interpretation of the Church* (Louisville: Westminster John Knox Press, 1993.

14. Sharon Daloz Parks, *Big Questions, Worthy Dreams: Mentoring Young Adults in Their Search for Meaning, Purpose, and Faith* (San Francisco: Jossey-Bass, 2000), xii.

Fictional narratives, actual vocations

In her most recent novel, *Gossamer,* Newberry Medal winner Lois Lowry again returns to the themes of vocation, memory, and community.[15] The narrative can be seen as a metaphor for a lively community of faith, in which people of all ages engage in mentoring one another to embody Christ for an aching world.

Littlest One is the newest member of a family-like group of creatures who practice the art of dream-making. They drift silently through the homes of sleepers, lightly touching photographs, buttons, quilts, and backpacks to soak up the memories stored there. At first, Littlest One is assigned to be mentored by Fastidious, but it soon becomes apparent that the young one's questions, curiosities, playfulness, and repeated small failures are too taxing for Fastidious. A new mentor is assigned, and so begins a lovely relationship in which Thin Elderly finds delight in the apprentice's blossoming gifts and gains new insights to the practice of dream-making through watching Littlest One, who bears an exquisitely light touch.

In the book's climax, Littlest One worries if she has enough strength to construct a dream powerful enough to keep the evil Sinisteeds — smelly hordes who bring nightmares — from a fragile boy, John, who is healing from abuse. After concocting a potent dream laced with laughter and lullaby in a way that only she could do, Littlest One is thanked for her good work and given a new name, Gossamer. This new name honors her signature gift — the floating, delicate, lighter-than-air way in which she gathers memories and bestows dreams. In this naming, the community claims her suitedness for the work she has found and toward which she so clearly devotes her passions.

At the end of each exhausting night's work, Gossamer and Thin Elderly retire to their welcoming Heap of fellow creatures to sleep, storing up energy and imagery for the next night's work. In time, Gossamer will be given a new house to inhabit at night, and it will come with a new instructor. Her gifts will continue to emerge, as new

---

15. Lois Lowry, *Gossamer* (New York: Houghton Mifflin, 2006).

needs among the human community bring out heretofore unknown abilities.

This portrayal of caring community engaged in practices of give-and-take, success and failure, work and restoration, entices us to re-imagine the communal spaces *we* inhabit. For Christians, one such space is called church. Church is not just a Heap where similar creatures fall exhausted at the end of hard labor. It is a place that holds power to call out our best selves.

Work in the world that draws on our deepest resources of imagination and reason, skillfulness and art, planning and improvisation is liberating, joyful, and mysteriously fulfilling. But it requires community. As we build and create, we need others who watch and reflect with us. As we mend what is broken or sow what is yet to be born, we thrive most when we have others with whom to rejoice over small victories and with whom to mourn our failures, be they retrievable fumbles or life-altering devastations. Wrapped into and within each cycle of activity and productivity in the world, we need a welcoming Sabbath Heap, a place to rest and restore, relax and receive the blessings of the day.

Embracing a vocational paradox: Companionship for a journey that can be made only by one's self

We see youth ministry as a companioned walk in which young people together with adults seek ways to offer their lives to an anxious, hurting world. Churches that catch this vision for youth ministry no longer try to compete with the entertainment industry for the attention and affections of young people. They need not understand the thriving of youth ministry in terms of the number of youth who come to the church basement to eat pizza on a Wednesday night. Instead, they find ways — sometimes with pizza included, sometimes not — to invite young people into practices of faith that live out their Christian callings. Throughout this volume we have referred to youth ministry in ways that stress community, the vital role of mediators of God's call, and the importance of adult companions who mentor youth in practicing their faith by walking with them. There exists a certain paradox, however, in the relationship of adults to the vocational journeys traveled by youth. Whether they are present as youth ministers, parents, teachers, coaches, or other adults who walk with young people, these adults are in the paradoxical position of accompanying young people on communally situated journeys that the youth in some sense must take alone. Here we do not refer to the aloneness of isolation, or the lack of companions on the journey. Rather, we mean that ultimately young people themselves must be the ones to respond to God's call and activate their gifts: no one else can make these decisions, dream these dreams, give these gifts, or feel these feelings for young people. In ministry with youth, we work to create spaces of hospitality to young people and to the spirit of God, spaces where young people can attend to such decisions, dreams, gifts, and feelings. These are spaces in which, as the prophet Joel long ago proclaimed, "It shall come to pass afterward that I will pour out my spirit upon all flesh, and your sons and your daughters shall prophesy. Your old men shall dream dreams, your young men shall see visions; and also upon the servants and upon the handmaids I will pour out my Spirit and they will prophesy" (Joel 7:28–29). May we, adults who care about young people and the world in need of their prophetic gifts, also be empowered by that same Spirit of God, as we join young people in the offering of our lives.

Epilogue

A conversation on youth and vocation
with James W. Fowler

On a blue-sky day in March 2006, we took a meandering walk through an Atlanta subdivision. We collected our thoughts on the work we had been doing and processed a recent round of life changes we had each endured. Lives are often in transition, and engaging with one another in reflection on our own vocational journeys had become a nice fringe benefit of our collaboration.

A few hours later, we were warmly welcomed into the home of James and Lurline Fowler. Jim, a long-time guide, mentor, and friend, is a person whose work weaves through every portion of this volume.[1]

We knew we needed his voice to be part of the conversation: his practical theological work on vocation and human faith development is pivotal, both immensely significant in the field of practical theology and also for framing some of our thinking about faith, vocation, and human personhood. *Stages of Faith* maps a theory for understanding how faith changes across the lifeline of human development. This pioneering work took seriously the developmental thinkers — Piaget, Erikson, Kohlberg. It brought them into conversation with Jim's own research and his theological understanding of the nature of faith, drawn from the theology of H. Richard Niebuhr and Paul Tillich. In recent years, developmental theories, including Fowler's faith development theory, have been critiqued as making features common to certain populations (e.g., males, college students,

---

1. James W. Fowler, *Stages of Faith: The Psychology of Human Development and the Quest for Meaning* (San Francisco: HarperCollins, 1995); *Faith Development and Pastoral Care* (Philadelphia; Fortress Press, 1987); *Becoming Adult, Becoming Christian* (San Francisco: Jossey-Bass, 2000).

European and Euro-Americans of the middle class) normative for all. Fowler's research did include both women and men, boys and girls, and he benefited from colleagueship with Carol Gilligan. He has remained open to new information, particularly feminist and minority voices and the way they critique "universal" stage theories.

We were thrilled when he agreed to read the volume and join us for a tape-recorded interview. Seated comfortably in his office-den, we invited his comments on vocation and youth ministry.

What follows is an excerpt from that spirited encounter, used with his blessing as this book's closing words. It points to the ongoing conversation we hope this book stimulates.

* * *

Dori: Did you, as a young person, experience vocation as a companioned walk?

Jim: I went to Lake Junaluska, a United Methodist conference center in western North Carolina, when I was in the eighth grade. It was a pivotal place in my journey. I was exposed to a lot of excellent preaching and teaching there. It was also at Junaluska that a man named Carlyle Marney came into my life. A liberal and progressive Southern Baptist pastor, he became a mentor to me. Early in our friendship he took me on a horseback ride in the Smoky Mountains. For the first time I talked with an adult male like I'd never done before. He was arguably the best pastoral theologian I ever knew. . . . Marney was the founder of Interpreters' House, a center for self-examination and growth in faith. I worked with him there, and it was in that context that I learned to listen to peoples' faith journeys. In my time with Marney I devoured the work of Erik Erikson, who helped me become a developmentalist. Marney died too soon; I never got to let him know what I did with what he gave me. I have an immense gratitude.

Joyce: With this background, you help us imagine the church as perfectly poised to help young people in the journey of vocation. Is it fair to argue this should be a primary task of youth ministry?

Jim: In this book you offer a new approach to youth ministry. Too often youth ministry has been framed as a train you get on that is already pretty well set and very controlling in some ways. You are clear that simply putting youth in good environments and trying to protect them from the evils of the world is utterly fruitless. By testimony and example, you are giving us depictions of the serious imagining and sensing and desires of young people to find a meaningful and grounded way of being in the world. You have confidence about relating to youth in a way that takes their growth and their nascent adulthood very seriously — and that also takes very seriously the fact that their gifts and the circumstances of their lives open them to the possibility of paths that are genuinely distinctive and faithful.

Dori: Do you think that alternative vision of youth ministry might feel threatening? Does it disrupt what we think of as youth ministry?

Jim: It's a great relief to those who are working with young people to know that it's not the gimmicks or the persuasiveness or the cleverness or the features of their being that recruits these young persons into faith. Instead, it is an adult availability to the young person in a triadic relationship in which you trust them, they trust you, and something else is involved. That something else is the Spirit of God. The Spirit has its own wisdom. We, like the youth, are involved in a trusting, faithful experiment that reaches toward genuine partnership with God, and to learn to make sense of a world in which God calls us to serve. They learn that we are not alone: We are *not* alone.

Joyce: In light of what you just said about the importance of a triad — youth, adults, and the Holy Spirit — what shape ought religious education with adolescents take?

Jim: It is a very imaginative kind of work that is called for and that you are crafting. Somehow, typically, when we get to doing religious education with adolescents, the imagination drops out in favor of control. "This is what you need to believe in confirmation in order to become a member of the church." Unfortunately, we do this right at the instant that they — developmentally — are ripe to shift into high gear in the cultivation of imaginative capacities. Religious education as a breeding ground for imagination is subversive because it works against predetermined and narrowing outcomes.

Dori: Can you speak more of your vision of the role of adults who companion youth in vocation? Are there adults who are bearers of hope?

Jim: There are very few paved roads in vocation. And so, the issue becomes one of creating paths or holding environments that are nurturing and encouraging, and yet open-ended. We need holding environments that provide places for discovering and testing hopes and capacities — places where it is safe to experiment, and also places that expose youth to people whose vocations are inspiring and genuine. These adults can then talk with youth about how their paths opened. I think to have adults who are committed and active, who talk candidly about how the spirit has worked in their lives, is a very important thing. Most adults, even Christians, don't claim the opportunity to talk about the strange quirks and the unanticipated ways in which the vocation they are living has taken form.

Joyce: Is there a way you articulate an understanding of vocation these days that makes more sense to you now, for this era?

Jim: I grew up in an era that was all too simple. You just gave your life to God and assumed it would all work out. That's obviously not adequate today! How are people navigating this complex world and trying to be faithful to it? How are they moved by the Spirit to expand beyond the promises of a late capitalist society? No wonder the time period we call adolescence now reaches well into the twenties in people's lives. It seems to me that the formative experiences for youth today have become fragmented and very, very complex. It takes a while for the cognitive and emotional capacities to address the wide range of experience and stimuli and wounds that they have experienced. It's a complex and protracted enterprise.

Dori: How does this change the developmental perspectives you helped construct?

Jim: These days I do find myself thinking differently about developmental perspectives like those I've articulated throughout my work. It certainly is clear that the holding environments that make possible the kind of development I tried to articulate in my work have become fragmented. The images and stories that bombard young people nowadays are many-faceted and ambiguous and enticing. The hustle and bustle is so fast, so pervasive. The stimulation from all our media is so overwhelming. The storing mechanisms and the space to interrogate yourself, and to be closely related to others that you can trust — these are all now harder to find.

Joyce: And yet young people are making sense of their worlds. . . .

Jim: What impresses me in relation to adolescents and young adults is how much more canny they are about these things than I would have been. I think they have a hermeneutics of suspicion that is almost built in. The question is how to create space where they can articulate to us and for us how they're making sense of the world, because they are. The model that you're offering is one that really honors that kind of complexity.

Dori: You've talked about your own mentor, Carlyle Marney, and how absolutely significant he was in helping you name and claim your vocational path as an adolescent. What evidence do you see of that kind of mentoring in the lives of boys and girls today?

Jim: We live in a time when compelling adult models are sorely lacking. We are fortunate that a literature now exists about adolescent girls, as both your work illustrates. A similar literature is now emerging about boys. But what models are there? Macho models of men have been utterly discredited. There are no clear models for what being a good man is in this time. We need a new round of thinking about how boys become men and what kind of men they become. We have bought the soft side and the gentle side. We don't often enough see the kind of courage and combativeness and challenge that men at their best can bring. I'm on the side of helping men widen expression and own it. As men, we're not given much space to try to assess and express our emotions. Our full humanity is inhibited by images of maleness and manhood.

Joyce: Where do you find hope?

Jim: I think this is a very difficult time for people to know how to live well. I'll confess it's hard for me to see how the Spirit is working in late capitalist United States. I can only hope for forces of renewal and of a more robust notion of what U.S. leadership in the world ought to look like. I hope for a new vision of what our investments in the really troubled parts of this world ought to be. I hope for visionaries to lead us. I think so much of our public life, including a lot our churches, is done in a survivalist hanging-on mode, rather than out of a sense of living into our fullness. The only group that is proactive is the advertisers and merchandisers, the creators of the next diversion. It is truly astounding how creative we are on the consumption side and how shortsighted we are on what really matters. My hope rests in Christian formation that witnesses to the long lines of convergent faithfulness and that can reframe and restore good faith in our public, religious and family dimensions.

Dori: What would that look like?

Jim: It comes down to an abiding trust in God's Holy Spirit. We are not alone. In this light, vocation makes sense. Our responsibility is vast, but it is limited. We can be what we are called to be in the drama of life, trusting that our faithfulness has consequence. When we can't manage, God can somehow find ways to make a way. Meaning comes in trying to find how your gifts contribute to the meaning of God's venture. This message invites us to the strong hope of facing a not-too-hopeful world. We need adult companions of youth to walk with them, study with them, work with them, and pray with them. Young people need adult Christian companions whose looking forward and witnessing to their faith offers a hope and commitment that contradicts a lot of what our culture teaches. The source of that is the Gospel story: living with hope rather than sight. It's a story we're called to teach and to live.

Bibliography

Adamson, Joni, Mei Mei Evans, and Rachel Stein. *The Environmental Justice Reader: Politics, Poetics and Pedagogy.* Tucson: University of Arizona Press, 2002.

American Association of University Women. *Girls in the Middle: Working to Succeed in School.* Washington, D.C.: AAUW, 1996.

———. *How Schools Shortchange Girls.* Washington, D.C.: AAUW, 1992.

Armour, Ellen T. "Essentialism." In *The Dictionary of Feminist Theologies,* ed. Letty M. Russell and J. Shannon Clarkson. Louisville: Westminster John Knox Press.

Baker, Dori Grinenko. *Doing Girlfriend Theology: God-Talk with Young Women.* Pilgrim Press, 2005.

Barth, Karl. *Church Dogmatics,* 4:3.ii. Trans. A. T. Mackay, T. H. L. Parker, Harold Knight, Henry A. Kennedy, and John Marks. Edinburgh: T. & T. Clark, 1961.

Bass, Dorothy, ed. *Practicing Our Faith: A Way of Life for a Searching People.* San Francisco: Jossey-Bass, 1997.

Bass, Dorothy, and Don C. Richter. *Way to Live: Christian Practices for Teens.* Nashville: Upper Room Books, 2002.

Bateson, Mary Catherine. *Composing a Life.* New York: Plume, 1990.

Belenky, Mary Field, Blythe McVicker Clinchy, Nancy Rule Goldberger, and Jill Mattuck Tarule. *Women's Ways of Knowing: The Development of Self, Voice, and Mind.* San Francisco: HarperCollins, 1986

Blodgett, Barbara. *Constructing the Erotic: Sexual Ethics and Adolescent Girls.* Cleveland: Pilgrim Press, 2002.

Bowers, C. A. *Educating for an Ecologically Sustainable Culture: Rethinking Moral Education, Creativity, Intelligence, and Other Modern Orthodoxies.* Albany: State University of New York Press, 1995.

Bronfenbrenner, Urie. *The Ecology of Human Development.* Cambridge, Mass.: Harvard University Press, 1979.

Brown, Lyn Mikel, and Carol Gilligan. *Meeting at the Crossroads: Women's Psychology and Girls' Development.* New York: Ballantine Books, 1992.

Brueggemann, Walter. "Covenanting as Human Vocation." *Interpretation* 33, no. 2 (1979): 126.

Buechner, Frederick. *Wishful Thinking: A Seeker's ABC*. New York: Harper & Row, 1973.

Calvin, John. *Institutes of the Christian Religion*. Ed. John T. McNeill. Trans. Ford Lewis Battles, in collaboration with the editor and a committee of advisers. Philadelphia: Westminster Press, 1960.

Celan, Paul. *Gesammelte Werke*, Frankfurt am Main. As quoted in Shoshana Feldman, and Dori Laub. *Testimony: Crises of Witnessing in Literature, Psychoanalysis, and History*. New York: Routledge, 1992.

Crain, Margaret Ann, and Jack L. Seymour. "The Ethnographer as Minister: Ethnographic Research in Ministry." *Religious Education* 91 (Summer 1996): 299–315.

———. *Yearning for God: Reflections of Faithful Lives*. Nashville: Upper Room Books. 2003.

Davis, Patricia. *Beyond Nice: The Spiritual Wisdom of Adolescent Girls*. Minneapolis: Fortress, 2001.

———. *Counseling Adolescent Girls*. Minneapolis: Fortress Press, 1996.

Dryfoos, Joy G. *Safe Passage: Making It Through Adolescence in a Risky Society*. New York: Oxford University Press, 1998.

Dykstra, Robert, with Allan Cole and Donald Capps. *The Spirituality of Boys: Losers, Loners, and Rebels*. Louisville: Westminster John Knox. 2007.

Elliot W. Eisner. *The Educational Imagination*. New York: Macmillan, 1979.

Erikson, Erik. *The Life Cycle Completed: A Review*. New York: W. W. Norton, 1982.

———. *Identity and the Life Cycle*. New York: W. W. Norton, 1980.

Fowler, James W. *Becoming Adult: Becoming Christian. Adult Development and Christian Faith*. San Francisco: Harper & Row, 1984.

———. *Faith Development and Pastoral Care* Philadelphia: Fortress Press, 1987.

———. *Stages of Faith: The Psychology of Human Development and the Quest for Meaning*. San Francisco: HarperCollins, 1995.

Gilligan, Carol. *In a Different Voice: Psychological Theory and Women's Development*. Cambridge, Mass.: Harvard University Press, 1982.

Gilligan, Carol, Nona Lyons, and Trudy Hanmor, eds. *Making Connections: The Relational World of Adolescent Girls at Emma Willard School*. Troy, N.Y.: Emma Willard School, 1989.

Gilligan, Carol, and Annie Rogers. "Reframing Daughtering and Mothering: Paradigm Shift in Psychology." In *Daughtering and Mothering: Female Subjectivity Reanalyzed*, ed. Janneke Van Mens-Verhulst, Karlein Schreurs, and Liesveth Woertman. New York: Rutledge, 1993.

Gilligan, Carol, Janie Ward, Jill McLean Taylor, and Betty Bardige. *Mapping the Moral Domain: A Contribution of Women's Thinking to Psychological Theory and Education*. Cambridge, Mass.: Center for the Study of Gender Education and Human Development, 1988.

Gilkey, Langdon. *Nature, Reality, and the Sacred: The Nexus of Science and Religion*. Minneapolis: Fortress Press, 1993.

Gurian, Michael. *The Good Son: Shaping the Moral Development of Our Boys and Young Men*. New York: Penguin, 1999.

———. *The Minds of Boys: Saving Our Sons from Falling behind in School and Life*. San Francisco: Jossey-Bass, 2005.

———. *What Stories Does My Son Need? Books and Movies that Build Character in Boys*. New York: Putnam, 2000.

———. *The Wonder of Boys: What Parents, Mentors, and Educators Can Do to Shape Boys into Exceptional Men*. New York: Putnam, 1997.

Hall, G. Stanley. *Adolescence: Its Psychology, and Its Relations to Anthropology, Sex, Crime, Religion, and Education*. New York: Appleton, 1904.

Harrington, Steve. "Developing a Biblical and Theological Foundation for Christian Wilderness Adventure Ministries." D.Min. Advanced Pastoral Studies Program. San Anselmo, Calif.: San Francisco Theological Seminary, 1998.

Hick, John. *A Christian Theology of Religions: The Rainbow of Faiths*. Louisville: Westminster John Knox, 1995.

Kegan, Robert. *The Evolving Self: Problem and Process in Human Development*. Cambridge, Mass.: Harvard University Press, 1982.

———. *In Over Our Heads: The Mental Demands of Moral Life*. Cambridge, Mass.: Harvard University Press, 1994.

Kindlon, Daniel J., and Michael Thompson. *Raising Cain: Protecting the Emotional Life of Boys*. New York: Ballantine, 1999.

Kolligian, J. J., and R. J. Sternberg. "Perceived Fraudulence in Young Adults: Is There an 'Imposter Syndrome'?" *Journal of Personality Assessment* 56, no. 2 (1991): 308–26.

Kovan, Jessica, and Dirkx, John.' "Being Called Awake': The Role of Transformative Learning in the Lives of Environmental Activists." *Adult Education Quarterly* (February 2003): 99–118.

Kvale, Steinar. *InterViews: An Introduction to Qualitative Research Interviewing*. Thousand Oaks, Calif., and London: Sage, 1996.

Lane, Belden. "Spirituality as the Performance of Desire: Calvin on the World as a Theatre of God's Glory." *Spiritus* 1, no. 1 (2001): 1–30.

LeGuin, Ursula. *Gifts*. New York: Harcourt, 2004.

Lines, Timothy Arthur. *Functional Images of the Religious Educator*. Birmingham: Religious Education Press. 1992.

Long, Thomas G. *Testimony: Talking Ourselves into Being Christian.* San Francisco: Jossey-Bass, 2004.

Lowrey, Lois. *The Giver.* Boston: Houghton Mifflin, 1993.

———. *Gossamer.* New York: Houghton Mifflin, 2006.

MacKinnon, M. H., and M. McIntyre. *Readings in Ecology and Feminist Theology.* Kansas City, Mo.: Sheed and Ward, 1995.

Mahan, Brian J. *Forgetting Ourselves on Purpose: Vocation and the Ethics of Ambition.* San Francisco: Jossey-Bass, 2002.

Males, Mike A. *Framing Youth: Ten Myths about the Next Generation.* Monroe, Me.: Common Courage Press, 1999.

March, Eugene. *The Wide, Wide Circle of Divine Love.* Louisville: Westminster John Knox, 2005.

McFague, Sallie. *The Body of God: An Ecological Theology.* Minneapolis: Fortress, 1993.

Mechling, Jay. *On My Honor: Boy Scouts and the Making of American Youth.* Chicago: University of Chicago Press, 2001.

Mercer, Joyce. "Gender, Violence and Faith: Adolescent Girls and the Theological Anthropology of Difference." Ph.D. diss., Emory University, 1997.

———. *GirlTalk on Faith and Families.* San Francisco: Jossey-Bass, forthcoming.

Merchant, Carolyn. *The Death of Nature: Women, Ecology, and the Scientific Revolution.* New York: Harper & Row, 1990.

———. *Earthcare: Women and the Environment.* New York: Routledge, 1995.

Miller, Alice. *The Drama of the Gifted Child: The Search for the True Self.* New York: Basic Books, 1997.

Moessner, Jeanne, ed. *In Her Own Time: Women and Developmental Issues in Pastoral Care.* Minneapolis: Fortress Press, 2000.

Moore, Mary Elizabeth. *Education for Continuity and Change.* Nashville: Abingdon Press, 1983.

———. *Ministering with the Earth.* St. Louis: Chalice Press, 1998.

———. *Teaching from the Heart: Theology and Educational Method.* Minneapolis: Fortress Press, 1991.

Parker, Evelyn L. *The Sacred Selves of Adolescent Girls: Hard Stories of Race, Class and Gender.* Cleveland: Pilgrim Press, 2006.

———. *Trouble Don't Last Always: Emancipatory Hope among African American Adolescents.* Cleveland: Pilgrim Press, 2003.

Parks, Sharon Daloz. *Big Questions, Worthy Dreams: Mentoring Young Adults in Their Search for Meaning, Purpose, and Faith.* San Francisco: Jossey-Bass, 2000.

Paulsell, Stephanie. *Honoring the Body: Meditations on a Christian Practice.* San Francisco: Jossey-Bass, 2002.

Pipher, Mary. *Reviving Ophelia: Saving the Selves of Adolescent Girls.* New York: Ballantine Books, 1994.

Pollack, William S. *Real Boys: Rescuing Our Sons from the Myths of Boyhood.* New York: Random House, 1998.

Pollack, William S., with Todd Shuster. *Real Boys' Voices.* New York: Random House, 2000.

Rabey, Steve. "Saving Kids from 'Nature-Deficit Disorder.' " *Youthworker Journal* (September–October 2005), online: *www.youthspecialities.com/articles/topics/cultural/naturedd.php?.* Access date 10/30/2005

Reis, F. M. "Internal Barriers, Personal Issues, and Decisions Faced by Gifted and Talented Families." *Gifted Child Today* 25, no. 1 (2000): 14–28.

Roehlkepartain, Eugene. "Connecting with Boys: Closing the Asset Gap." *Assets: The Magazine of Ideas for Healthy Communities and Healthy Youth* (Summer, 2001), accessed on-line at *www.search-institute.org.* Access date 12/12/06.

Rogoff, Barbara. *The Cultural Nature of Human Development.* New York: Oxford, 2003.

Rosenthal, Michael. *The Character Factory: Baden-Powell and the Origins of the Boy Scout Movement.* New York: Pantheon Books, 1986

Ruether, Rosemary Radford. "Ecofeminism and Theology." In *Ecotheology: Voices from the North and South,* ed. David G. Hallman, 199–204. Maryknoll, N.Y.: Orbis Books, 1994.

———. *New Woman, New Earth: Sexist Ideologies and Human Liberation.* Minneapolis: Seabury, 1975.

———. *Women and Redemption: A Theological History.* Minneapolis: Fortress Press, 1998.

———. *Women-Church: Theology and Practice.* San Francisco: Harper & Row, 1986.

Russell, Letty M. *Church in the Round: Feminist Interpretation of the Church.* Louisville: Westminster John Knox Press, 1993.

Schuurman, Douglas J. *Vocation: Discerning Our Callings in Life.* Grand Rapids, Mich.: William B. Eerdmans, 2004.

Smith, Christian, with Melinda Lundquist Denton. *Soul Searching: The Religious and Spiritual Lives of American Teenagers.* New York: Oxford University Press, 2005.

Smith, Yolanda. *Reclaiming the Spirituals: New Possibilities for African American Christian Education.* Cleveland: Pilgrim Press, 2004.

Steere, Douglas V. *Gleanings: A Random Harvest.* Nashville: Upper Room. 1986.

Tappan, Mark B., and Martin J. Packer, eds., *Narrative and Storytelling: Implications for Understanding Moral Development*. San Francisco: Jossey-Bass, 1991.

Turpin, Katherine. *Branded: Adolescents Converting from Consumer Faith*. Cleveland: Pilgrim Press, 2006.

Warren, Michael. *Seeing through the Media: A Religious View of Communications and Cultural Analysis*. Harrisburg, Pa.: Trinity Press International, 1997.

———. *Youth, Gospel, Liberation*. San Francisco: Harper & Row, 1987.

Way, Niobe, and Judy W. Chu, eds. *Adolescent Boys: Exploring Diverse Cultures of Boyhood*. New York: New York University Press, 2005.

Westerhoff, John. *Will Our Children Have Faith*. Rev. ed. Harrisburg, Pa.: Morehouse, 2000.

Wimberly, Anne Streaty. *Soul Stories: African American Christian Education*. Nashville: Abingdon Press, 1994.

Yust, Karen Marie. "Creating an Idyllic World for Children's Spiritual Formation." *International Journal of Children's Spirituality* 11, no. 1 (2006): 182.

Index

Vocation (*continued*)
  work or career choice and, 62,
    156–58, 161
  youth contribution to church's
    theology of, 155–56, 161,
    164–65, 167, 171
Worship, 1, 10, 35, 57, 68
Youth ministry
  alternative vision of, 6, 10–11,
    50, 62, 178

Youth ministry (*continued*)
  contemplative/holy listening as
    work of, 70, 79–85
  focused on vocation, 50, 67
  uses of nature in, 55–61
Youth Specialties, 56
Youth Theology Initiative, ix, 7, 35,
  36–39, 41, 53, 63, 69, 73, 74,
  80, 85, 113
Yust, Karen Marie, xii, 58–59